Praise for *A Call From Heaven*

"*A Call From Heaven* is an extraordinary compilation of personal accounts and high-caliber research into what is commonly known as 'deathbed phenomena.' Josie's warm and welcoming personality makes her the perfect confidant for people with spiritually intimate events to share. The cumulative weight of these cases and the scientific inquiry that it inspires make a compelling case for the hypothesis that our consciousness and personal identities do not conclude with the death of our physical bodies. The stories are heartfelt and often nothing short of amazing. Reading this bold and poignant work leaves us solidly convinced that there is an eternal dimension to human life and a gorgeous horizon to which we can fearlessly proceed when our time on this earthly stage has drawn to a close."
—Cassie McQuagge, director of Support Services & Outreach, Edgar Cayce's Association for Research and Enlightenment (ARE)

"Josie Varga's new book *A Call From Heaven* reminds us that our consciousness continues after death. The stories of those close to death reveal the peace and grace that is present when we pass from this life. It does us good to hear these stories so we understand that we do not cease to exist when we cross over. Josie has included accounts of pre-death awareness from doctors, nurses, and many individual accounts as well as information from leading researchers in the field. I highly recommend this valuable and rewarding book."
—David Bennett, author of *Voyage of Purpose* and
A Voice As Old As Time

"Varga beautifully illustrates how *A Call from Heaven* is a common experience that is transformative. Her wide-ranging stories of deathbed visions and after death communication may well awaken the memory of such experiences in the readers' minds and make them alert to future contact from deceased loved ones. Readers are likely to have a decreased fear of death through encountering incidences of survival of consciousness after death. For all of us, this understanding may well transform our world view through changing our ideas about the meaning of death in our lives."

—Pamela M. Kircher, MD, author, *Love is the Link*

"Step into the pages of this beautifully written book and you will see why the stories are precious gifts from Heaven. Both informative and profoundly inspirational, *A Call from Heaven* speaks to us in hushed and holy voices, and in warm and gentle tones. It is impossible not to be moved, often to tears. I love this book and would highly recommend it!"

—Nancy Clark, national award-winning author, *Hear His Voice, Divine Moments, My Beloved*, and *Stop Trying to Fix Me*

"Combining solid scientific and medical research with moving and emotional personal testimonials, *A Call From Heaven* offers undeniable evidence of what we may experience at and after death. This book educates, empowers, and inspires us to look beyond our fears of the unknown to recognize that what we perceive as an ending can truly be a beginning. Author Josie Varga has done an amazing job of offering one of the most comprehensive and fascinating books on the subject. A must-read that will change your perception of what it means to die."

—Gary Mantz and Suzanne Mitchell, co-hosts, Mantz and Mitchell, 1150 KKNW Seattle

A CALL
FROM
HEAVEN

Personal Accounts of
DEATHBED VISITS, ANGELIC VISIONS,
and CROSSINGS TO THE OTHER SIDE

JOSIE VARGA

New Page Books
A Division of The Career Press
Wayne, NJ

A Call From Heaven
Edited by Gina Schenck
Typeset by PerfecType, Nashville, Tennesee
Cover design by Amy Rose Grigoriou
Birds image by Mrs. Opossum/shutterstock
Cover background image by Konstanttin/shutterstock
Printed in the U.S.A.

To order this title, please call toll-free 1-800-CAREER-1 (NJ and Canada: 201-848-0310) to order using VISA or MasterCard, or for further information on books from Career Press.

The Career Press, Inc.
12 Parish Drive
Wayne, NJ 07470
www.careerpress.com
www.newpagebooks.com

Library of Congress Cataloging-in-Publication Data

CIP Data Available Upon Request.

DEDICATION

This book is dedicated in loving memory of my godmother
Lucy LoBrace; my maternal grandmother, Josephine Oliveri;
my uncle Tony (Sabato Tropeano); and my cousin Angelina Southern.
When my time comes to join you in Heaven, I have no doubt you
will be there to guide me to the Other Side. I love and miss you all.

ACKNOWLEDGMENTS

Brian Tracy, a well-known entrepreneur and author, once said "The more credit you give away, the more will come back to you. The more you help others, the more they will want to help you." This book is a testament to his wise words. My heart-felt gratitude goes out to all those who made *A Call From Heaven* possible.

Thank you to Dr. Peter Fenwick and his wife, Elizabeth. I am forever grateful to have the backing of one of the most respected authorities in near-death research. Thank you for taking the time to write the foreword. If you ever need my help, I am here for you both.

To the many who offered their expert testimony, words cannot express what it means to me to have your trust and support. Thank you Carla Wills-Brandon, PhD; Dr. Penny Sartori; Dr. Michael Barbato; Shelley E. Parker; Ineke Koedam; Annie Cap; William Peters; Eben Alexander, MD; Dr. Steve Taylor; Dr. Joan Borysenko; Dr. Betty Phillips; Dr. Bruce Greyson; Dr. Alexander Batthyany, PhD; and Pamela M. Kircher, MD. It is truly and honor and a privilege to work among such a respected group. Thank you for your important work.

This book would not have been possible without the many contributors who agreed to share their experiences in the hopes of helping others understand that life does continue. Thank you all so very much.

I am obliged to my primary-care physician, Dr. Toro, for making me realize that this book needed to be written. I am also grateful to my publisher, New Page Books. Thank you for your belief in both me and this book.

I would be remiss if I did not mention a wonderful, talented young girl named Emily Sorrentino. Emily worked for me as an intern and her help proved to be invaluable as we made final edits to this book. Thank you, Emily.

Lastly, I want to acknowledge my family and friends. This book proved to be a huge undertaking. Thank you for your patience and understanding as I spent countless hours at the computer. Thank you to those of you who never wavered in your support and love, especially my husband, John, and daughters, Erica and Lia. I love you so much.

CONTENTS

Foreword by Dr. Peter Fenwick 13

Introduction 17

Comatose to Lucid Right Before Death 25

The Question of Consciousness: Dr. Eben Alexander
and Dr. Steve Taylor 30

One Last Hug: Carla Wills-Brandon, PhD 38

Chuck, I'm Coming 45

Two Blankets for a Boy and a Girl 46

My Son Ken 48

Yes, I'm Ready 50

"Peak in Darien" Experiences: Dr. Bruce Greyson 52

Understanding the Dying Process: Penny Sartori, PhD 56

Shankar 63

I Keep Seeing People 65

A Soul Departing? 67

Will I Go to Heaven? 67

Life's Mysteries Are Revealed in Its Final Moments:
Dr. Michael Barbato 68

Mistakes Are Made in Love's Service: Dr. Joan Borysenko 72

A Patient Named John Loranger 78

I Will See You at 9 O'clock 79

The Angel of Death 81

Prophetic Dreaming: Shelley E. Parker 83

It Wasn't a Dream 91

She Would Get There When She Got There 93

She Nodded Three Times 94

In the Light of Death: Ineke Koedam 95

Who Is in the Back of the House? 100

Aunt Terry 102

I Don't Want to Go 103

Dying to See Angels: Dr. John Lerma 105

Take My Hand 111

Send Me Pink Roses 112

Nonna 113

A Shared-Death Experience 115

My Sister Came for Dad 124

A Visit in the Intensive Care Unit 127

Who's There? 130

Atmospheric Changes 131

My Mother Appeared Before My Eyes 134

A Mother's Love 137

Aunt Verna 139

Dream Visits 140

He Has Never Let Me Down. 142

Well, Hello, Everett!. 143

A Message for His Wife 144

Ethel Mary Kates Tennis 146

A Joyous Musical Reunion 147

Yellow Roses for Nancy 150

Final Gifts: Dr. Betty Phillips 154

Spiritual but Not Religious. 157

NDEs in Terminally Ill Patients Differ From Those
in Acute Events: Dr. Pamela M. Kircher 161

Final Thoughts. 169

Appendix: There Is Life After Death 175

Bibliography. 177

Notes 181

Index 185

About the Author 191

Death is no more than passing from one room to another. But there is a difference for me you know, in that other room, I shall be able to see.
—*Helen Keller*

FOREWORD

What is the meaning of life? Why are we here? What happens when we die? Every culture has its own answers to these questions, which reflect the views of the society in which they live. Some require acts of faith, some are formed from myths and legends; all are based on belief structures of one kind or another. The lack of any belief structure may result in a nihilistic attitude, which often results in an intense fear of death itself.

But we now live in a scientific era in which belief is not enough. What is demanded, if a belief is to be taken seriously, is evidence. And until recently, the scientific evidence suggested that consciousness was limited to the brain, and that nothing survived the death of the brain; the continuation of consciousness after death in any form was impossible. But more recently there has been an awakening within our culture saying that there is evidence for phenomena that simply do not fit easily into the scientific paradigm that limits consciousness to the brain. The science of consciousness is, at the moment, in its infancy, but it has demonstrated already the necessity to look at death more closely and the beginning of a realization that death is merely a part of life; by ignoring the evidence that suggests even a faint possibility that some form of consciousness may survive it, we impoverish the world we live in—and may indeed impede our own scientific progress.

The best evidence for what happens as we die must surely come from the dying themselves. And that is why Josie Varga's book is so timely. She has talked to physicians and researchers, to caregivers and friends, who have all worked with or been close to the dying, and gives us numerous accounts of how those who are dying view their own experiences. It is particularly significant that, although many people close to death show huge disruption in their brain and body functioning, the experiences they talk about are almost always lucid, occurring in clear consciousness, and having the authenticity of truth rather than the stigma of confusion.

How do we know that these accounts are not just stories that those close to death imagine in order to try to elaborate a future for themselves? Why should we accept that these are genuine experiences rather than the desperate attempt of a failing mind to give logic and meaning to their last hours? One reason is their consistency and the similarity of the pattern they follow. For example, the unexpected appearance of "visitors" (usually dead relatives) at their bedside, and the comfort and reassurance such visits bring, both to the dying and their relatives. This book records many such experiences, so numerous and so convincing that it is impossible to doubt the sincerity of those who report them. The sheer weight of this admittedly anecdotal evidence seems to support their truthfulness and emphasize the importance of our own understanding of death.

As Freud said, when we talk about death, we're prepared to talk about other people's death, never our own. In the time of our Victorian ancestors no family could hope to escape death easily. Most children had experienced the death of a sibling; death was an everyday event that could not be denied. Nowadays, even in the medical profession, we have gotten into the habit of sweeping it under the carpet, regarding it simply as our own failure to prolong life.

But dying, if only we allow ourselves to look at it, is a very special time. Of course for the dying person and his or her family, it will inevitably be a difficult time, but many find answers in a very personal and direct way to questions that they may never have asked before.

Josie Varga's book will help give more perspective to the way we understand death and help return it to its rightful position as a very significant and important part of life, and help us to realize that by accepting death, we enrich both ourselves and our culture. Her book should leave no one with any doubt that the experiences she describes are not rare. They are not even unusual. I am willing to bet that if in a gathering of friends, relatives, or colleagues, you ask anyone if they have had a similar experience, a few hands will go up. Just try it and see.

Dr. Peter Fenwick
Author, *The Art of Dying*
Researcher and internationally renowned neuropsychiatrist

I still live.
—Last words of Daniel Webster

INTRODUCTION

In April 2012, I went to my family doctor for an annual physical. Dr. Toro is a wonderful, highly respected physician and we always end up having enlightening conversations about the work both he and I do. He asked me if I was working on any more books and I told him about my book, *Divine Visits,* which is about divine and angelic encounters. I noted that another doctor said he is noticing spiritual experiences now more than ever before. Dr. Toro looked at me and not surprisingly said, "I know. He's right." He then went on to share an experience that just happened that same week:

> We were getting ready to transport a patient of mine to another hospital for experimental treatment. We could not do anything more for her at our hospital. My patient, however, told me that it was her time. I was in the hospital room along with other family members at the time. She happily told everyone that her grandson (who was killed in the Iraq war) was there in the room. She even carried on a conversation with her grandson while everyone in the room watched in amazement.

I asked Dr. Toro if he felt his patient was hallucinating (knowing full well that she wasn't). My doctor looked at me smiling and said, "No, I don't. She was perfectly coherent. She even joked with her friend who was in the room telling her that she couldn't marry her husband. She then looked up and told her grandson that she was ready," he continued. "A few minutes later, she passed. There are things that we will never be able to fully explain. But I can tell you that seeing this made it so much easier on her family."

I went on to explain that this experience was known as a deathbed visit and how common they actually are. Unfortunately, many doctors feel that these phenomena cannot be explained, but in my opinion, they can be. Spirit is primary and the physical is secondary. We are not of the body. Consciousness is outside the brain. We are all part of this Universal Consciousness. This Consciousness is made up of energy, which cannot be created or destroyed. The very atoms from which our physical bodies are made are energy. So, in short, we always were and we always will be.

That day after leaving Dr. Toro's office, I decided that I needed to research deathbed phenomena, and this book was born.

Deathbed Visits Throughout History

Deathbed visits (DBVs) are far more common than most people realize. They have been reported throughout history and across different cultures and religions. One of the first recorded deathbed visits was by an eighth-century English historian named Bede. He told the story of a dying nun who was visited by a deceased holy man. He told her that she would die at dawn, and according to the account, she did.

Deathbed visits and other paranormal phenomena were considered normal and not taboo. It was common for people to die in the comfort of their own home and, therefore, more frequently witnessed by family members and friends. These deathbed visits are still happening; the difference is they are occurring, more often than not, in hospitals and nursing homes.

Although many are now being reported and there is certainly more acceptance in medicine and science, many go unreported. The number-one reason for this is fear. The dying are afraid people will think they are crazy and those who care for them are afraid to be ridiculed by their peers. It is said that at no time are we more honest than when we are on our deathbeds. If only more people would listen to the stories of the dying, we would know what our ancestors knew a long time ago. We would finally understand that they provide evidence in not only our survival after death, but also realize that we are far more than the physical body.

Although these experiences have taken place since the beginning of time, they were not methodically studied until the 20th century by a British physicist and psychic researcher named William Barrett. His specific interest in deathbed visits was triggered by an experience that his wife had in 1926. His wife, Florence E. Barrett, an obstetrician, was deeply affected by a patient, Mrs. B., who died shortly after giving birth. The following is Lady Barrett's account of what happened:

> Suddenly, she looked eagerly toward one part of the room, a radiant smile, illuminating her whole continence.
>
> "Oh, lovely, lovely," she said.
>
> I asked, "What is lovely?"
>
> "What I see," she replied in low, intense tones. "Lovely brightness, wonderful beings." It is difficult to describe the sense of reality conveyed by her intense absorption in the vision.
>
> Then, seeming to focus her attention more intently on one place for a moment, she exclaimed, almost with a kind of joyous cry, "Why, it is Father! Oh, he's so glad I'm coming; he is so glad. It would be perfect if only W (her husband) could come too."
>
> Her baby was brought for her to see. She looked at it with interest, and then said, "Do you think I ought to stay for baby's sake?" Then turning toward the vision again, she said, "I can't, I can't stay; if you could see what I do, you would know I can't stay." She turned to her husband, who had come in, and said, "You won't let baby go to anyone who won't love him, will you?" Then she gently pushed him to one side saying "Let me see the lovely brightness." I left shortly after, and the Matron took my place by the bedside. She lived for another hour, and appeared to have retained the double consciousness

of the bright forms she saw, and also of those tending her at the bedside; she arranged with the Matron that her premature baby should remain in hospital until it was strong enough to be cared for in an ordinary household.[1]

What amazed Sir Barrett most was what the Matron said later on. Shortly before her death, Mrs. B. told her husband and mother (who was also in the room with them) that her sister Vida was there. Vida had passed away three weeks prior, but Mrs. B. was never told of her sister's death. Yet, she insisted that her sister was there along with their deceased father.

The founder of the Society for Psychical Research, Barrett conducted his study of what he termed "deathbed visions" from 1924 to 1926. Countless stories were recorded from around the world, but the strongest evidence in the validity of these accounts comes from those who, like Mrs. B., named people whom they did not know were dead at the time.

In yet another account, Barrett tells the amazing story of two friends named Jennie and Edith who were both stricken with diphtheria. Jennie passed away on a Wednesday afternoon but the family did not want Edith to know that her friend was gone.

The following Saturday, Edith asked to have two photographs sent to Jennie, but still nothing was said of her friend's death. That evening, Edith became very ill and began to say goodbye to everyone. Suddenly, to everyone's shock, she exclaimed, "Why, Papa, I am going to take Jennie with me! Why Papa, you did not tell me that Jennie was here." She then reached out her arms and said, "Oh, Jennie, I'm so glad you are here!"[2]

Some doctors still may claim that these deathbed visits are the result of hallucinations. In cases such as these, that theory doesn't hold up and it doesn't make sense. How is it possible for the dying to name people whom they didn't know were deceased? There is no other logical explanation than to say that these experiences are real.

Although there are some similarities between hallucinations and these deathbed phenomena, there are also some remarkable differences.

HALLUCINATIONS	DEATHBED VISITS
Fearful and confusing	Comforting and peaceful
Psychotic	Coherent and consistent
Not spiritually transformative	Transformative, lasting impact
Occur during states of paranoia	Can occur minutes, days, weeks, and even months before death
Nonrealistic	Truthful/realistic
Cannot be shared	Can be shared

Hallucinations are also not typical of deceased relatives. Carla Wills-Brandon explained this when she wrote:

If DBVs are just the result of the dying brain, oxygen depriva-tion, neurosis, or chemical imbalances, why are most of the visions of people who are deceased? Why do these visions typ-ically involve not just visions, but visitations from the Other Side? If DBVs were hallucinations or the result of random fir-ing of brain synapses, why are the themes of these visions so consistent with one another? Hallucinations from one person to the next are not this consistent. The by-product of random firings of the brain produces chaotic visions, not consistent encounters with deceased relatives.[3]

When such behaviors are hallucinatory, they can generally be controlled by medication. However, these deathbed visits cannot be controlled. They occur regardless of whether or not the patient is medicated.

In yet another study carried out by the Society for Psychical Research, parapsychologists Karlis Osis and Erlendur Haraldsson studied thousands of deathbed phenomena in both the United States and India. Of those studied, 50 percent were found to have experi-enced some type of deathbed visit, and they were also found to be very similar from one culture to another. Most of the subjects died within 10 minutes after their vision or experience.[4]

A different study was conducted at the Center for Hospice and Palliative Care in Cheektowaga, New York, between January 2011 and July 2012. The study was done by Christopher W. Kerr, MD; Pei C. Grant, PhD; James P. Donnelly, PhD; Debra Luczkiewicz, MD; and other colleagues. Daily interviews were conducted with 66 patients (59 were included in the analysis). It was the first study to examine deathbed phenomena from the patients' point of view instead of doctors, nurses, hospice workers, family members, and so on. At the conclusion of the study, a total of 453 interviews were completed.

- Ninety-nine percent said the experience appeared to be real.
- Nearly half of the dreams or visions occurred while the patient was asleep.
- The most common vision involved deceased relatives and friends.
- The most common theme was the need to prepare for a journey and noting that deceased loved ones were waiting.
- These experiences diminished the fear of death and brought comfort to the dying.[5]

It is estimated that between 50 and 60 percent of conscious dying patients experience some form of deathbed visit. However, the number is predicted to be much higher, as only about 10 percent of all dying patients are conscious. Plus, it is also important to remember that many such experiences go unreported by either the patient or others involved for fear of being ridiculed and judged.

Other surveys I've found have put the number of the dying experiencing these phenomena as high as 77 percent, as well as the number of those witnessing them at 65 percent. But as noted, it is impossible to come up with an exact number because many go unreported.

William James was one of the most influential philosophers of the 19th century, but what some don't realize is that he also studied metaphysics, religion, and the idea of an afterlife. "To upset the conclusion that all crows are black," he said, "there is no need to seek demonstration that no crows are black; it is sufficient to produce one white crow; a single one is sufficient."[6] Perhaps, then, exact numbers are not important. What is, however, is the fact that these deathbed phenomena actually occur. I've found many times in my research that people want to speak privately about their experience, but don't want it made public. I wish I had a dime for every time someone came up to me and said, "Josie, this is just between me and you." Some consider the experience divine and personal.

People approach me everywhere I go once they know that I am an afterlife researcher. I remember once I went to a friend's house and she introduced me to her sister-in-law. At the time, I was working on my book *Visits to Heaven*, which features near-death experiences (NDEs) from around the world. When her sister-in-law heard about my book, she proceeded to tell me about a NDE she had experienced while giving birth. I was amazed by the details of her story and asked her if she would allow me to share it in my upcoming book. She said, "Josie, that experience was sacred to me. I feel like it was between me and God and shouldn't be shared."

Many believe that these deathbed visits provide us with one of the most compelling proofs of life after death. Although *deathbed visions* or *departing visions* are more commonly used terms, these deathbed phenomena will be referred to as *deathbed visits* in this book. My reasoning is simple: These occurrences are not always visual. At times, those on their deathbed may hear angelic music and voices. So the experience may be solely auditory.

The following are some of the most common forms of deathbed visits (DBVs):

1. **Visual:** Seeing deceased relatives and friends; seeing angelic or religious figures such as angels, Jesus, and the Blessed Mother.

2. **Gateway:** Witnessing the opening of a portal in which the dying see glimpses of Heaven or the Other Side.
3. **Atmosphere:** Room changes, such as temperature, and physical anomalies, such as the appearance of bright light or mists leaving the body.
4. **Synchronicity:** Unexplainable occurrences such as clocks stopping at the time of death or phones ringing.
5. **Dreams:** Dreams that announce the impending death.
6. **Auditory:** Hearing what many on their deathbed describe as angelic or Heavenly music.
7. **Shared:** The visit is also witnessed by others either in the room or long distances away.

Deathbed visits are powerful metaphysical experiences that the dying may experience before death. The dying may be visited by deceased loved ones, strangers, or angelic or divine figures. Religious beliefs appear to have no bearing on these experiences because even atheists and nonbelievers have reported such phenomena. At times these visits are experienced by others in the room, offering incredible validity to the idea that life truly does continue in some form. In most cases, those who are visited on their deathbed are told that their visitors have come to assist them in their transition to the Other Side. We'll never know how many of these mystical experiences go unreported, but one thing is for sure: They are clearly underestimated, yet cannot be easily discounted. If only there was greater awareness of these deathbed phenomena, the dying, their family and friends, and those who care for them could be better prepared when the time does come and ultimately find peace and comfort in knowing that life does continue.

James Anthony Froude, a 19th-century English historian and novelist, once wrote: "We enter the world alone, we leave the world alone."[7] As the saying goes, I beg to differ. As this book will show you, we are never really alone. Not in birth. Not in life. And certainly not in death.

Comatose to Lucid Right Before Death

Terminal lucidity, seen time and time again, is a term used to describe the unexpected return of mental clarity and responsiveness shortly before death in those who were previously incoherent.

One of the most amazing cases on record is Anna Katharina Ehmer (1895–1922), a severely disabled woman who lived in a mental institution. University of Virginia Researchers Bruce Greyson, MD, and Michael Nahm, PhD, explore Ehmer's case in a paper published in *Omega—Journal of Death and Dying*.

Ehmer never spoke a word her entire life but, according to reports, this changed on her deathbed when she shocked doctors by singing songs for 30 minutes prior to her death. The head pastor, Friedrich Happich, was asked to join Dr. Wilhelm Wittneben at Ehmer's bedside. When the two men entered the room, they were shocked by what they witnessed. "When we entered the room together, we did not believe our eyes or ears," wrote Happich. "Kathe, who had never spoken a single word, being entirely mentally disabled from birth on, sang dying songs to herself. Specifically, she sang over and over again, 'Where does the soul find its home, its peace? Peace, peace, Heavenly peace!' For half an hour she sang. Her face, up to then so stultified, was transfigured and spiritualized. Then she quietly passed away."[1]

Both Happich and Wittneben wrote similar accounts of what happened. In fact, they pointed out that Ehmer had never given them any indication that she was even remotely aware of her environment. "From birth on, she was seriously retarded," according to Happich. "She had never learned to speak a single word. She stared for hours on a particular spot, then she fidgeted for hours without a break. She gorged her food, fouled herself day and night, uttered an animal-like sound, and slept."[2]

According to skeptics who have reviewed this case, the fact that Ehmer did not speak her entire life does not prove that she couldn't speak. Perhaps, they speculate, she chose not to speak. I tend to agree with the skeptics because it is difficult to authenticate these reports from almost a century ago. However, the idea that such a story would be identically fabricated by two respected individuals doesn't make sense.

Also, this account of terminal lucidity taken in conjunction with those that have since been reported only gives it more credibility. People with Alzheimer's disease and schizophrenia with severely impaired mental workings have suddenly regained intellectual clarity shortly before death.

The majority of neuroscientists have, up until now, asserted that once the brain is damaged, normal mental reasoning and perception becomes impossible. But new research suggests that this is not necessarily always the case.

Professor Alexander Batthyany, PhD, teaches courses in behavioral science and philosophy at the University of Vienna in Austria. At the time of this writing, he is currently conducting a large-scale study on terminal lucidity in those stricken with Alzheimer's disease. Thus far, his preliminary findings suggest that normal cognition can occur despite a severely damaged brain. However, his research has found that this only occurs when a person is near death.

Conventional science has no explanation for this. Professor Batthyany has called these deathbed phenomena "close to a miracle," however, he admits, "I am not sure whether miracle is a good word, but it is deeply mystifying given what we know about the relationship between mental function and brain integrity."[3]

I then questioned him about why he decided to undertake such a study.

> Why do I study this? How could I not? The day I heard about this phenomenon, I was surprised that so few people look into it. In the beginning, I was slightly skeptical whether I would find cases. Now, I have so many that I wonder how I will be able to cope with all the data which need to be analyzed. . . . There is a growing database which seems to point to a far more complex picture of the relation between brain, mind and self than we tend to assume.[4]

Professor Batthyany has conducted several other research projects and his impressive work has been cited in numerous books and publications. In another paper he authored, "Complex Visual Imagery and Cognition During Near-Death Experiences," he studied cases of enhanced conscious awareness and visual imagery during near-death experiences. The results of this study were published in the *Journal of Near-Death Studies* in 2015, in which he writes, "Together with case studies of terminal lucidity and mindsight, our findings of enhanced mentation and visual imagery during severe physiological crises appear to therefore indicate that, at least near death, the relationship between cognition, perception, and their neuronal correlates might be more complex than traditionally thought."[5]

As an example, Alzheimer's disease kills nerve cells and tissue in the brain. Through time, those affected by the disease lose almost all of their normal brain functions beginning with memory loss. Although someone stricken with Alzheimer's, schizophrenia, or any other mental disorder may suddenly become coherent on their deathbed there are no observable changes in the brain. In other words, the nerve cells in the damaged brain don't suddenly become alive and allow communication to take place.

The brain doesn't suddenly fill up with new neurons. The brain remains exactly how it was prior to the terminal lucidity taking place.

This means that conventional science is incomplete and additional research certainly needs to be conducted. In addition, according to "Terminal Lucidity: A Review and a Case Collection," published by researchers at the University of Iceland and the University of Virginia, "Several of these accounts suggest that during terminal lucidity, memory and cognitive abilities may function by neurologic processes different from those of the normal brain. We expect that significant contributions to better understanding the processes involved in memory and cognition processing might be gained through in-death studies of terminal lucidity."[6]

One of the more recent remarkable cases is reported by Dr. Scott Haig, a New York–based orthopedic surgeon. In 2007, Dr. Haig chronicled a patient named David, who died from lung cancer, in the *TIME* article "The Brain: The Power of Hope." His body was so filled with cancer that it spread to his brain. In fact, Haig noted, there was barely any brain left at all, leaving him both speechless and motionless.

> The cerebral machine that talked and wondered, winked and sang, remembered jokes and birthdays and where the big fish hid on hot days, was nearly gone, replaced by lumps of hap-hazardly growing gray stuff. Gone with that machine seemed David as well. No expression, no response to anything we did. As far as I could tell, he was just not there.[7]

The day after his patient passed way, Dr. Haig was approached by a nurse who had cared for David on his deathbed. According to Dr. Haig, the nurse told him that David miraculously woke up and proceeded to say goodbye to his family. She went on to explain that he was lucid and alert as he talked to his family for about five minutes. David then passed out once again before dying within the hour.

At first, Dr. Haig did not know what to think, but two weeks later he had his answer when he ran into David's wife, Carol, who happened to be a nurse at the same hospital. When asked if what he had heard was true, Carol nodded and said, "Oh, yes, he sure did."[8]

Haig had no reason not to believe her, but states what awoke David that day was not his damaged brain but his mind. The two, he believes, are separate. At this point, David's brain at was damaged and basically nonexistent. "Tumor metastases don't simply occupy space and press on things leaving a whole brain," Dr. Haig noted. "The metastases actually replace tissue. Where that gray stuff grows, the brain is just not there."[9]

So, if his brain was "just not there," and David was still able to wake up and converse with his family, wouldn't that seem to indicate that consciousness is outside of the brain?

In conclusion, Dr. Haig wrote, "I fix bones with hardware. As physical as this might be, I cannot be a materialist. I cannot ignore the internal evidence of my own mind. It would be hypocritical. And worse, it would be cowardly to ignore those occasional appearances of the spirits of others—of minds uncloaked, in naked virtue, like David's goodbye."[10]

We cannot ignore the evidence. Just because we may not understand how something is possible doesn't mean that it is nonsense and it doesn't mean it didn't happen. In western Bolivia, stands a famous ancient archaeological site known as Puma Punku. The site contains examples of engineering that are far beyond present-day understanding. Stones weighing several tons are meticulously placed and have no chisel marks.

The stones, it was discovered, came from two different locations miles apart. How is it possible without modern transportation and machinery? Also, close examination of these huge stone blocks reveals that they were interlocked in three dimensions, which makes them strong enough to withstand earthquakes and other volcanic activity. How this was even possible remains a mystery but, again, this does not change the fact that it happened. We may not understand how, but they are real.

Likewise, we may not understand how these deathbed visits and other spiritual phenomena are possible, but they are there. They are happening. And they are real.

The Question of Consciousness

Dr. Eben Alexander and Dr. Steve Taylor

The discussion of terminal lucidity brings up an important question: If a person who has suffered severe neurological damage and has been comatose for an extended period of time can suddenly communicate, what, then, is consciousness? That is, if David's brain had been destroyed and, as Dr. Haig put it, "is just not there," is consciousness then outside the brain?

Recently, my husband and I dropped our daughter Erica off at her friend's house. While there, I struck up a conversation with her mother and the topic turned to my books. Her friend's older sister Rachel was intrigued. When I mentioned that my latest book would discuss the topic of consciousness and whether or not it is outside the brain, Rachel chimed in, "How do you know it's not a little bit of both?"

Rachel, an honors student and high school senior, explained that she has always been fascinated by the workings of the brain and plans on becoming a neuroscientist. (I look forward to seeing her contributions to science someday.) Rachel really got my own brain thinking: What if consciousness is both inside and outside of the brain? What if it is, as she put it, a little bit of both?

Consciousness is our perception of the world around us. Simply put, it encompasses our thoughts, our memories, our feelings, and so on. It is what we regard as our reality. Hence, it makes sense that one of the biggest puzzles in science today is whether or not consciousness is a product of the brain or if the brain is somehow a receiver of consciousness. The implications of this question are astounding.

If consciousness is not dependent on the brain, then it can continue without the physical body. If it can continue without the physical body, then consciousness continues after death. If consciousness continues after death, it would suggest that there is life after death.

Daegene Song, a South Korean quantum physicist, claims he has mathematically shown that consciousness arises outside the brain. Although the brain does access our consciousness, such consciousness is not generated by it. "Among conscious activities, the unique characteristic of self-observation cannot exist in any type of machine. . . . Human thought has a mechanism that computers cannot compute or be programmed to do. . . . The brain and consciousness are linked together, but the brain does not produce consciousness. Consciousness is something altogether different and separate."[1]

Song claims to have generated mathematical evidence that consciousness cannot be simulated by a computer—not now, not ever. No matter how large the computer brain, it will never be self-aware. If consciousness was part of the brain then the opposite would be true: It could be replicated by a computer, according to Song. Since this is not the case, he believes that consciousness is not generated by the brain.

Part of the problem with the question of consciousness is that many try to explain it in material terms. I don't believe that you can explain consciousness as such. In fact, I don't believe you can explain deathbed phenomena or other mystical phenomena satisfactorily in physical terms. If you believe that consciousness is produced by the brain, then when the brain is dead so is consciousness. However, if you believe that consciousness is outside of the brain and the physical body, then it is possible to understand how awareness continues on after death.

Dr. Eben Alexander

On November 10, 2008, Dr. Eben Alexander, a well-known, highly respected academic neurosurgeon, contracted an E. coli infection that put him in a coma for seven days. As a result, the outer layer of his brain (the neocortex)—the area of the brain that controls thought and emotion—was shut down. "When your brain is absent, you are absent, too," he writes in his groundbreaking book, *Proof of Heaven.*[2]

Dr. Alexander learned more about the true nature of reality and consciousness during those seven days in a coma than he did in his many years of schooling and medical practice. "The more my scientific mind returned, the more clearly I saw how radically what I'd learned in decades of schooling and medical practice conflicted with what I'd experienced, and the more I understood that the mind and the personality (as some would call it, our soul or spirit) continue to exist beyond the body," he writes.[3]

His near-death experience changed his outlook completely. Previously, he would have said if you don't have a working brain, you can't be conscious. Like most of his medical colleagues, he believed that the brain was responsible for producing consciousness. No brain, no consciousness. However, even though Dr. Alexander's neocortex was shut down, he was still conscious and aware. In fact, he says, he visited a realm (Heaven) that was "almost too real to be real."[4] It was a beautiful place of peace and love.

Nowadays when asked about consciousness he will admit he had it all wrong. The brain does not generate consciousness; rather, it acts as sort of a filter for consciousness. Death of the body and the brain is not the end of consciousness or life. Even though Dr. Alexander spent more than three decades perfecting and fine-tuning his scientific view of reality, everything changed after spending seven days in a coma. Even though his brain was not capable of producing thoughts or dreams, he was very much conscious and aware.

Dr. Alexander further explains his views on consciousness by saying that consciousness is primary and generates everything else. "Consciousness is the thing that exists. The spirit and the soul also exist and are eternal. The mystery is in better defining how consciousness interacts with the physical world."[5]

One thing Dr. Alexander said is very clear:

Consciousness (soul/spirit/divinity) creates the brain and all of physical reality, not the other way around. The emerging scientific view is of the brain as a reducing valve or filter that limits primordial consciousness down to the apparent trickle of the here-and-now that we experience in our mundane daily physical existence. The most important consequence of this emerging scientific view is that when our brain and body die, our conscious awareness is actually liberated to a much higher form.[6]

When asked what the message was that he hoped to share as a result of his experience, Dr. Alexander said: "Our souls are eternal; we do not need to fear death. Life does not end with the physical body."[7]

Although everything appears to be separate, this is only an illusion. As Dr. Alexander will tell you, we are truthfully all interconnected, loved deeply and unconditionally.

––––––––

Dr. Steve Taylor

The author of several best-selling books on psychology and spirituality, Steve Taylor, PhD, is also a senior lecturer at Leeds Beckett University. He has made *Mind, Body, Spirit* magazine's list of "the 100 most spiritually influential living people" for the past four years. His articles have been published in more than 40 academic journals, magazines, and newspapers.

In his article "The Puzzle of Consciousness," he explains why we need to not only think outside the box when examining consciousness but "outside the brain." The following is reprinted with his permission.

Over the last 20 years, the field of consciousness studies has become increasingly popular, partly because some scientists believe that consciousness is one of the last remaining mysteries. According to this narrative, we have now reached the point where we largely understand problems like evolution, the nature of life, and the origins of the universe, so now it's time for us to turn our attention inside and solve the problem of consciousness.

Consciousness is difficult to define, partly because it's us. But most definitions of consciousness include two elements: our subjective experience (that is our thoughts, feelings, perceptions, and sensations—or qualia as they are sometimes collectively called), and our awareness of the world around us and the phenomena and processes which take place in it. When scientists began to investigate consciousness, most were confident that it wouldn't be too long before the mystery would be solved. They believed that brain-scanning technologies would enable us to see how billions of the brain's neurons work together to produce our subjective experience. However, despite more than two decades of intensive research and theorizing, very little (if any) progress has been made. Originally, neuroscientists thought that consciousness would be located in a specific area of the brain, then tentatively suggested that in some way it seems to emanate from the brain as a whole. However, no one has any idea how this might occur.

It might seem natural to assume that consciousness is produced by the brain—as a scientist once said to me, "We don't have anywhere else to look. If consciousness doesn't come from the brain, where else could it possibly come from?" However, this argument is strikingly similar to the arguments which were once commonly used to support the existence of God— "There's no other way of explaining it, so it must be God!"

In fact, some philosophers have suggested that the assumption that the brain produces consciousness cannot possibly be true. The brain is just a soggy clump of gray matter—how could that soggy mass possibly give rise to the richness and depth of consciousness? To think that it could is a "category error"—the brain and consciousness are distinct phenomena, which can't be explained in terms of each other. As the philosopher Colin McGinn has put it, to say that the brain produces consciousness is like saying that water can turn into wine.

Famously, the philosopher David Chalmers called this the "hard problem." Psychologists and neuroscientists can understand some problems fairly well—e.g., how the mind process information, how attention and memory operate, and so on. These are the "easy problems." But the "hard problem" of how the brain might produce consciousness is much less amenable to explanation, and may be completely insoluble.

However, there are viable alternative ways of explaining consciousness besides through brain activity. David Chalmers's own view is that, rather than produced by the brain, consciousness may be a fundamental force of the universe, like gravity or mass. In this way, consciousness came into being when the universe began, and exists everywhere and in everything. A similar view is put forward by the philosopher Robert Forman, who suggests that consciousness exists as a kind of field, outside the brain, and that the function of the brain is to "pick up" consciousness, like a radio receiver, and then to "channel" it into our individual organism.

To me, this model makes more sense than to continue hammering away fruitlessly at the brain for an explanation of consciousness. It also makes more sense than to explain away consciousness as an illusion—as Daniel Dennett does in *Consciousness Explained*, for example (where he suggests that qualia don't really exist, and that in reality there is no one "in" our brains looking out at the world). The idea of consciousness as a fundamental force is strikingly similar to the outlook of many of the world's indigenous peoples. Completely independently, many indigenous groups developed concepts of a fundamental "spiritual force" which they perceived as pervading the whole of reality. In America, the Hopi called it *maasai*, the Lakota called it *wakan-tanka*, and the Pawnee called it *tirawa*, while the Ufaina (of the Amazon Rainforest) call it *fufaka*. The Ainu of Japan called it *rambut* (translated by the anthropologist Monro as "spirit-energy"), while in parts of New Guinea it was called *imunu* (translated by early anthropologist J.H. Holmes as "universal soul"). In Africa the Nuer call it *kwoth* and the Mbuti call it *pepo*. As these peoples perceived it, this force is not a personal being such as a deity, who watches over the world and requires human beings to worship it. It is usually seen as an all-pervading force or power, with no gender or personality.

This view of consciousness has a great deal of explanatory power in other areas. It helps to explain human compassion, empathy and altruism, for example. Altruism makes little sense from a materialist point of view, since we're all individual beings enclosed in our bodies, and the primary aim of our lives is to sustain our own well-being. It makes no sense for us to put the well-being of others before our own, or to go out of our way to help strangers, or members of other species. But if consciousness is a fundamental force or a field, then in a sense it's something we all share, or participate in. It's therefore possible for us to empathize with other people, to experience their own sufferings as if they are our own, and to feel a desire to alleviate them. In a sense, other people's sufferings are our own.

This model is also consistent with telepathy. Telepathy also makes no sense at all from a materialist point of view, which is why many materialists are so keen to dispute research suggesting that it's a real phenomenon. But again, if consciousness is a fundamental force, we shouldn't be surprised if telepathy is real. There is a fundamental connection between living beings—a shared network of consciousness through which information could be exchanged from unit to unit.

This "radio" model also fits with an argument which is often used in favour of the idea that consciousness is produced by the brain: Damage to the brain would still affect or impair consciousness, just as damage to a radio would impair its broadcast of programmes.

So, in explaining consciousness, it may be that we literally need to think outside the box—that is, outside the brain. We are not just conscious—in a sense, we are consciousness, and consciousness is expressing itself through us. And in that sense, we all share the same consciousness.[8]

Having studied spiritual phenomena for more than a decade now, I agree that there may be some things we never understand about consciousness. However, there is one thing that I do know: Consciousness cannot be inside the brain. As my daughter's friend Rachel speculated, it might be a little of both. This makes sense if the brain accesses consciousness but does not create it. It cannot be entirely inside the brain but the two are clearly linked.

At the moment, you are reading this book. Your mind is sensing the page in front of you, not inside of your head. Therefore, your awareness or consciousness of this book is outside, not inside your head. Everything that we experience, we experience outside the brain.

So if everything that we experience, our consciousness of everything around us, is outside the brain, does that mean that our thoughts create our reality? Yes, it does. This is one of the key principles of quantum physics. In the early 1900s, scientists set out to prove this with the famous double-slit experiment. Some of the world's greatest minds have referred to this experiment to explain how consciousness is dependent on the observer.

In other words, this study demonstrated that the behavior of energy is determined by the awareness of the observer. A double-slit visual system was used to test particles at the quantum level. What they found was astounding: At times, electrons would act as particles. Yet other times, under the same conditions, these electrons would act as waves. Simply put, the very observation of these electrons controlled the outcome. Consciousness, therefore, shapes the nature of our reality.

Quantum physics discovered that everything in the universe is made up of energy. Yes, matter may look solid. However, when we break matter down to its smallest observable level, we discover that it is energy. Consciousness and everything around us are connected to that energy. And as the double-slit experiment clearly demonstrated we can change matter and hence the universe simply by the way we observe it.

Renowned inventor and physicist Nikola Tesla once said, "The day science begins to study non-physical phenomena, it will make more progress in one decade than in all the previous centuries of its existence." Well said. The day we make the greatest achievements in understanding consciousness is the day we realize that science and spirituality are part of the same, single reality.

For information about Eben Alexander, MD, visit *www.eban alexander.com*. For information about Steve Taylor, PhD, visit *www .stevenmtaylor.com*. Daegene Song's paper can be found at *https:// arxiv.org/pdf/0705.1617v1.pdf*

One Last Hug

Carla Wills-Brandon, PhD

Carla Wills-Brandon, PhD, opens her book *One Last Hug Before I Go* with the unforgettable story of a trip to the grocery store with her youngest son, Joshua. He informed her, quite matter-of-factly, that they had another passenger in the car—a red-haired kid named Damus.

Not able to see this passenger supposedly sitting with her son in the backseat, Wills-Brandon asked Joshua who Damus was and how long he had been around. Her son surprised her by answering, "Oh, he's just some kid from the sky . . . he just got here! He came here for Da."

What makes this story remarkable is that "Da" was the name her two sons affectionately called their grandfather, who was in the hospital and not doing well. Shortly after this experience, Wills-Brandon's father-in-law passed away and the visits from Damus ceased.

At the tender age of 16, Wills-Brandon lost her mother to breast cancer. On the night that her mother passed, she awoke from a deep sleep, knowing intuitively and without a doubt that her mother was transitioning at that very moment. A feeling of sadness enveloped her as she ran downstairs to wait by the phone. What she didn't know then was that two good family friends had also been awakened in two separate locations miles away from the hospital.

Fifteen minutes after she woke up, the phone rang. The caller confirmed everything that Wills-Brandon and two others had been sensing: Her mother had just passed away. Years later, two other family members shared that they had been woken up as well. In total, five people in different locations felt Carla's mother's touch as she moved on from this life.

At that time, Wills-Brandon had no idea that she would later go on to become one of the world's leading researchers and authorities on deathbed phenomena. She is also a licensed marriage and family therapist and the author of 13 books, which cover a wide variety of topics, including intimacy, self-esteem, grief, the afterlife, and more. With more than 30 years of experience, she is a sought-after lecturer, both in the United States and abroad, and has appeared on numerous TV and radio programs.

To say that I am honored to have Carla Wills-Brandon in this book is an understatement. Besides our work with afterlife research, she and I share another similarity: Wills-Brandon, like me, has always wanted to be of service to others and to write. As I've said many times, helping others is what life is all about. When I'm on my own deathbed, I hope to look back at my life and say that I made a difference.

The fact that I'm able to combine this with my love of writing is a huge bonus. As for Wills-Brandon, she has already helped people in more ways than she'll ever know. She generously took the time to answer some questions.

How long have you been researching deathbed or departing visions? What led you to research this phenomenon?

I have been researching departing visions for 30 years. I've had contact all my life, but this began with my own departing visions as a youth. In spite of the experiences surrounding my mother's passing, her death was traumatic, so I poured alcohol and pills on top of this. When I found my own recovery and healing, I then got into the field of trauma. As a trauma specialist I've lectured across the United States and in parts of the United Kingdom and Europe. My husband and I worked Flight Medicine for NASA when the Space Shuttle *Challenger* blew up, along with other disasters. And working with trauma, I came across more departing visions. So, as I continued to do what I was doing with trauma, I slowly put these accounts away. I'd been told by my professional peers that it wouldn't be appropriate for me to discuss these experiences because it would ruin my career as a trauma specialist. When my son had an encounter at the age of 3, I decided it was time for me to break the silence. And that's when I began writing books on the topic. Three of my 13 books discuss departing visions.

One thing that researching afterlife communication has taught me is that we are so much more than the body. If we weren't, such spirit communication would not be possible. What have you learned from your research?

We come into the material world to learn. As spirit in material form we learn things that we wouldn't otherwise learn in the spirit world. This is for our growth. So there are challenges and lessons for us to be had. But at the same time, we're also supposed to recognize how we can create that afterlife existence here in the material world. When we've cleaned up the wreckage of our own past, our addictions or traumas or losses, along with our unresolved grief, then we can open up to spirit. We must first make peace with ourselves, our family and friends, and community before jumping into the exploration of after-life matters. After doing this, we can then begin our spiritual explora-tion and learn the importance of service to others. Making peace with family, past friends, and lovers who have harmed us doesn't always mean inviting them back into our lives. What this means is that it is essential that we heal our resentments, losses, fears, shame, and more. So we are here for a purpose.

You've heard hundreds of departing vision accounts. Are there any that stand out?

I've collected over 2,000 first-hand departing vision accounts. So many of them are special to me, but I'm going to share one about my husband. My husband is a meat and potatoes sort of guy. With a PhD in clinical child psychology and coming from a family of Holocaust survivors, he didn't want to have much to do with my exploration into departing visions, or, as a matter of fact, anything to do with the after-life. Then his father became very ill. He was incredibly close to his larger-than-life World War II physician father. Pop actually went back to Europe to rescue the relatives from the horrors of the Holocaust after the war and after liberation. The two were thick as thieves. One evening my husband decided to spend the night at his father's bed-side. While he was sitting there, holding his father's hand, he began to notice a pastel vapor was rising from his chest. It was a swirling colorful mist. I have numerous accounts like this and have seen this mist, but he'd never experienced anything like this before. Because he'd been married to me for so long, he knew what was going on. This really changed how he looked at life after death. And today, he goes to

Lily Dale, New York, with me every summer. Lily Dale is home to the Spiritualist movement in the United States.

Why do you think it's important that we continue to research spiritual or paranormal experiences such as deathbed visits?

We live in a very death-phobic society. About 100 to 200 years ago when someone was getting ready to pass the entire family could be found camped out around the bed, including the pets. Messages from the Spirit World would be discussed and questions would be openly asked. Children would also be at the deathbed. And so death wasn't seen as frightening, but instead as a part of the fabric of life. There was an experiential knowing that we moved from one existence to another. Unfortunately, with the fear of aging we have created generations of individuals who are scared to death of death. Young people I work with come in carrying the death phobia of their parents. As a licensed marriage and family therapist and a licensed clinical psychological associate, I work with lots and lots of individuals who are very death phobic. Once they receive information about departing visions the burden and fear begins to lift. We owe it to those that we serve to continue to investigate departing visions in order to turn the tide of death phobia that's so entrenched in our society.

I've found that many have a hard time talking about their experiences. They are willing to speak privately, but not publicly. Do you feel that more are willing to share now compared to when you first began your research?

People from many different countries and all walks of life have been approaching me for the last 30 years with their departing visions. When they find out I understand, there's a sense of relief. Interestingly, they always find it necessary to first qualify, letting me know they are perfectly sane, raising families, and working jobs. But when I share with them they are not alone, and here is the evidence, relief washes over them. Such validation gives them the courage and the strength to go back out there and share their incredible experiences with family and friends.

These deathbed visits offer amazing proof in the validity of the afterlife. What kind of an effect do DBVs have on the family and friends who witness them?

Departing visions release one from the bondage of fear about physical death and ideas like "hell." We learn, with consistent evidence, there is more after this. With such knowing, aging loses its sting. We can't learn how to fully experience enjoyment in our lives if we are constantly running from fear. Fear stunts creativity and blocks spirituality, so having understanding about afterlife matters is essential.

Can you explain what happens during and after a DBV based on your research?

For me and my research, I've found that there are some consistent themes with departing visions, but I'm going to just mention a few. What happens in these situations is that a visitation from the afterlife lets family members, friends, professional healthcare workers, and the individual who is getting ready to pass all know that we continue. Life continues. Such encounters relieve any sense of death phobia for both the individual who is getting ready to cross over, and for those at the bedside.

Those in the afterlife who are continuing their spiritual evolution and growth come to comfort us, lessen our fear, and offer us a "glimpse" of the world to come. This is a consistent takeaway theme, from one experiencer to the next. The other theme involves love.

Relationships aren't severed with physical death. Instead, the bonds of love continue. For those who are passing there is a reunification with friends and loved ones in an afterlife experience. With the evaporation of fear of death, some then turn their concerns to those who will remain, reassuring surviving loved ones that they will be okay and death is nothing to fear. Those who remain, the survivors, are often times visited by their loved ones. Before their death, they come in spirit form, in dreams, or with a knowing. Saying I love you, giving out hugs or words of comfort, they might talk about going on a trip. Or there can be what's called an empathetic departing vision where the individual who will survive experiences the emotions or physical sensations the individual crossing over is experiencing. It all boils down to having an understanding that the spirit continues.

Deathbed visits are all different yet so much alike. What are some of the most common elements? How do they differ?

I have three books on this topic. All different types of departing visions are discussed. I am sure that you have come across similar encounters and that these will fill your book. That said, I stand on the shoulders of those who have come before me. Departing deathbed vision researchers Dr. Peter Fenwick, Dr. Erlendur Haraldsson, and Dr. Raymond Moody are all acquaintances of mine. They and others have provided a foundation for my own investigations and I will forever be grateful. Before them there was Sir William Barrett and others who risked their professional reputations to explore this phenomenon. Credit must be given where credit is due.

What we all have found is that those preparing to transition, who have departing visions, have incredibly similar experiences. There may be an initial premonition of an upcoming time for departure, or a visitation with deceased loved ones. Visions of mists may appear or even a spirit body double. Music, flower scents, and more can also accompany such encounters. As a clinician I work with those who have hallucinations resulting from mental illness. From patient to patient, each hallucination is different. With departing visions the accounts are consistent, regardless of illness, age, sex, medication, religion, or lack thereof. My acquaintances in this field have also discovered these commonalities and are also convinced the contact is real.

Is there anything that I have not asked you that you would like to add?

As I continue to research and investigate and publish on departing visions and other afterlife matters, I recognize that my primary purpose is to present this information to individuals who are suffering with death phobia. My job is to be there for the individual who has had a departing vision or other afterlife encounter, and doesn't know where to turn to. I'm not supposed to go out there and make a big name for myself, but instead work with one individual at a time, sitting with them, while holding their hand, letting them know that their experiences are real.

In my practice I have individuals who have suffered from severe trauma. Extreme loss. And, as a consequence, they've become involved with drugs or alcohol or other addiction. Some are suicidal or very self-destructive. Tucked away in the recesses of their mind often times is an afterlife experience. Once the trauma has been cleared away, their addictions are in check, self-destructive behavior is put aside, and the emotions of rage, shame, and pain have been addressed, then we can look at these afterlife contacts. Such encounters can then provide the building blocks for continued spiritual growth. This is my purpose, to facilitate healing. And this is what I am dedicated to.

For information about Carla Wills-Brandon, PhD, visit *www.carla willsbrandon.com.*

 ## Chuck, I'm Coming

Mary Landberg, Oregon

Jack was dying from brain cancer and in the last days of his life. His entire family was in Boston at the time, and he was alone in Oregon. I sat quietly with Jack; only he and I were in the room. He was unaware of his surroundings and drifted in and out of consciousness.

He was having a delightful conversation with (an unseen) Chuck. It all started with an emotional plea for forgiveness, then shifted to laughter about old times spent down by the creek making mud pies to throw at their little sisters when they walked home from school. Then suddenly, with reverence, he said, "Chuck, I'm coming."

Later that day I called his sister in Boston and asked her who Chuck was. She told me Chuck was his best friend in high school. At 17, Jack stole his father's truck and took a midnight joy ride with Chuck in the front seat next to him. There weren't seat belts back then. So when Jack swerved to miss their neighbor's dog, he hit a tree and Chuck went partially through the windshield and bled to death while Jack watched helplessly. This would explain the huge scar Jack had across his face and down his neck. This would also explain his emotional plea for forgiveness.

The dying often see their deceased friends or parents and tell them with elation they are on their way. Family members can be alarmed when the dying start speaking out loud to loved ones who have passed before them. Was Jack's conversation with Chuck related to his brain tumors? Was he just confused? Or was Jack speaking his truth?

Does it really matter either way? If they don't feel alone, then they aren't alone.

In addition to being a hospice nurse, Mary Landberg is an accomplished photographer and author. Her book, *Enduring Love*, features a compilation of hospice portraits and stories documenting the final steps in life's journey. For more information, visit *www.marylandberg.com* or *www.hospiceportraits.com*.

Two Blankets for a Boy and a Girl

Santina, New Jersey

My friend Denise was diagnosed with ALS (amyotrophic lateral sclerosis), or what often is referred to as Lou Gehrig's disease. It was very painful to watch her slowly decline until finally she was in a coma and unresponsive. Some weeks prior, she started knitting a blanket—baby blue and orange, each strand of yarn so full of her love. A hospice nurse at the hospital had taught my friend how to knit. Denise began working on the blanket, but she unfortunately never got to finish it.

One day after she had slipped into a coma, I had gone to see her in the hospital. I spent some time with my friend and then went to the family waiting room, where I met the hospice nurse who told me all about the blanket, saying she felt it was such a shame that my friend didn't get to finish it. Later, I went to see Denise again and say my goodbyes before making my way to the elevator. With me, once again, was my friend's hospice nurse. As the nurse was talking to me in the elevator, I suddenly heard Denise's voice.

I heard her loud and clear as though she was standing right next me. She said, "Santina, tell her that you will finish the blanket for me. Tell her to give you everything and that you will finish the blanket for me." At first, I was startled to hear her voice, but not wanting to disappoint my friend, I quickly uttered, "Umm, give me everything. I will finish the blanket for her."

The nurse looked at me, somewhat surprised by my words, and I can tell you that I was surprised by my own words as well. "What?"

I looked at the nurse and repeated, "Give me what she did and the rest of the yarn and I will make sure that the blanket is completed and give it to her family. I think I need to do this for her."

Luckily, she did not argue with me and quickly agreed to give me what my friend had started. I honestly had no idea how to knit. I only knew that I had to do this for my friend.

Sadly, my friend never came out of the coma and died the next day. Not knowing who else to go to or what else to do, I went to visit my mother. My mother could not see well and wasn't in the greatest health, but, like I said, I didn't know who else to go to for help. I explained what happened and asked if she could please finish knitting the blanket. She agreed.

It took my mother a while to complete, but she finished knitting a beautiful blanket for a baby boy. However, when I went over to see the blanket, my mother stunningly informed me that she wasn't done. "Something is telling me to knit another one," she told me. "I have to knit another blanket for a baby girl."

To be honest, I was shocked by my mother's words. "What are you talking about, Mom? It's okay. One blanket is enough."

My mother, however, was not easily swayed and insisted that she knit another blanket. Six months after my friend's passing, both blankets were completed and I gave them both to her daughter Jeanine.

Another three months went by (nine months after my friend's death) and I received a phone call from Jeanine's husband; it was a call that I shall never forget. Jeanine was pregnant with twins. Yes, a boy and a girl.

My friend may have been unresponsive on her deathbed, but she found a way to get a very important message to me. A message that proves beyond a doubt that there is no death. Life does continue. Our loved ones are always around.

 ## My Son Ken

Rebecca, California

My son passed away on the evening of July 6, 2012. I had passed out from complete exhaustion. That night, I had the most vivid dream that I can still remember in explicit detail.

In the dream, I walked into my bedroom and Ken was sitting in the chair. I ran toward him and shrieked, "I knew you wouldn't leave me!" My son stood up just as I got to him, put his arms around me, and said, "Mom, I'm gone."

I cried, saying, "Please, please, you know I can't live without you here. Please come back." In response, he looked straight into my eyes and said, "I will be back to visit but not for a long time. She said I have a lot of work to do." We then hugged and he told me he loved me and was gone.

I woke up to my daughter asking me who I was hugging, as nobody was there. The reason I know this was not a dream is because, before my son passed away, the words "a lot of work to do" in correlation with passing on was not a thought in my head. My son's death is the first that I've experienced and never have I ever delved into the spirit realm, afterlife, and so on. I had no thoughts about it whatsoever. Since my son's passing, I've read everything I can about the afterlife and have tried to convince myself that he exists somewhere, but it's hard for me to grasp.

My mother became ill a few months later in late October. She was hospitalized that January and knew going into the hospital that she would not leave again. We all thought that she would bounce back as she always had, but that would not be the case.

The days leading up to her passing, I watched my mom as she became very frightened of death. Truthfully, as she neared the end, I don't believe she was ready to leave her husband or the rest of the family. When my son Ken passed, my mother was shattered. They always were extremely close and would talk to each other once or twice a week. The bond between them really was incredible.

A couple of days before my mother passed, I came to visit her and she said, "Kenny's been here." She said it so calmly as though it was completely natural. At first I thought it was all the medicine that she was on, but she was still lucid enough to recall memories of my childhood. So I knew this wasn't the case.

I asked her what he was doing and if she talked to him, and she replied, "No, he's just standing there against the wall smiling. I think he's waiting for me." The last day my mom could speak (prior to hospice arriving and starting the morphine drip in her arm) she said, "Kenny is here. He's waiting for me. He keeps smiling at me but he's not saying anything. Just like he's waiting for me."

She then went on to tell me that her mom was there as well; she passed in 1981. I believe my son was there to guide his grandmother into the next realm. My hope is that they are together watching over us.

At that time, my youngest son, Nathan, was on a three-month trip to Australia. My mom had paid for Nathan's trip and made him promise before he left that, should anything happen to her, he would not return home early. I tried to reach him several times to let him know that his grandmother passed away, but I could not reach him.

Nathan called me instead, however, to tell me about a dream he had the night my mother crossed over—unbeknownst to him. In the dream, he said he saw my mom and Kenny walking hand-in-hand on the beach in Australia. Perhaps this was their way of letting us all know that, yes, they are together and, yes, they are watching over us.

 ## Yes, I'm Ready

Cindy Bigham, South Carolina

On February 9, 2002, I lost my son Michael. The following year, on October 31, he came to me in a vivid dream. In the dream, Michael was driving a red sports car and pulled up to my paternal grandmother's house. When I saw him, I asked in surprise, "Michael, what are you doing here?" In response, my son told me that he had come to get "Mama" but she wasn't ready yet. He then said he would come back to get her when she was ready.

A few weeks later, I was telling my father about the dream and he looked at me with this strange expression on his face. Although he didn't explain why at the time, he told me to call my grandmother (his mother) and ask her about her dream. When I did I was surprised to learn that she, too, dreamt about Michael on the exact same day.

She said it was Halloween and she was out of candy. That night she dreamt that Michael came driving up to her house in a red sports car. She noted that he was wearing a grey sweater and khaki pants.

Interestingly, these were in fact the clothes he was buried in, yet my grandmother did not make it to his funeral and we never discussed what he was wearing with her.

Michael, according to my grandmother, then said, "Mama, are you ready yet?" In response, she told her great-grandson that she was not ready because she had to take care of a few things first. He then hugged her and walked away.

What I found equally astonishing was that Michael appeared with two little girls in both mine and my mother's dreams. Both girls had long dark hair. Although they did not say anything, they made their presence known to us.

My grandmother and I both knew who they were, however. I lost a daughter at birth in 1986, while Michael's girlfriend miscarried a baby at seven months pregnant in 2001. The girls appeared the same way to both of us in the dream and we instinctively knew who they were without being told.

After this experience, my grandmother told me that she felt her time was near and that she would try to prove life after death to me. She told me to take a picture of her casket at the funeral when that time came. On New Year's Eve, my dad had a feeling that something was wrong and went to see her. As he predicted, she was very sick and had to be taken to the hospital by ambulance. Sadly, my grandmother was found to have lung cancer.

Just two short weeks later, she went into a coma. The hospital allowed her to go home on February 25 and she was released to home hospice care. Two days later, she suddenly woke up from her coma, looked around the room, and smiled, saying, "Well, hey Michael, I see you're here like you said you would be." She then spoke to her deceased husband (my grandfather) saying, "Hey George, I have missed you for so long." He had passed away many years earlier in 1987. She then simply said, "Yes, I'm ready."

With that, she peacefully took her last breath and passed away. At her viewing, I got out my camera and took a picture of her casket as she had suggested. In the picture, you can clearly see a beam of white light coming into her casket. She said she would try to prove life after death to me and she did.

Death is only an illusion;we do continue to live.

"Peak in Darien" Experiences

Dr. Bruce Greyson

Thus far, we've highlighted various deathbed phenomena that offer convincing evidence that consciousness does indeed survive death. But perhaps the greatest proof comes from those that have come to be known as "Peak in Darien" cases after an 1882 book by the same name. Frances Cobbe, the author, discusses cases in which those on their deathbeds mention the presence of a deceased person of whose death they had no knowledge.

Cobbe took the title from a poem written by John Keats in which he describes the surprise of the Spaniards who, after reaching a peak in Darien (now in Panama), expect to see land. Instead, to their shock, they see another ocean.

Her book mentions several end-of-life experiences and she expresses surprise that such phenomena had not been studied in greater detail.

That "Peak in Darien" which we must all ascend in our turn—the apex of two worlds, whence the soul may possibly descry the horizonless Pacific of eternity—is the turning-point of human hope. And it appears to me infinitely strange that so little attention has been paid to the cases wherein indications seem to have been given of the perception by the dying of blessed presences revealed to them even as the veil of flesh has dropped away. Were I permitted to record with names and references half the instances of this occurrence which have been narrated to me, this short essay might have been swelled to a volume.[1]

In writing this book, I agree with Cobbe. Although research has certainly increased throughout the years, much more needs to be done before these spiritual phenomena even come close to being accepted by mainstream science. Countless incidents have been reported and cannot be easily discounted.

In a paper entitled "Seeing Dead People Not Known to Have Died: 'Peak in Darien' Experiences," Dr. Bruce Greyson, director emeritus of the division of perceptual studies, department of psychiatry and neurobehavioral sciences, University of Virginia Health System, argues that Peak in Darien experiences provide "persuasive evidence for the survival of consciousness after bodily death."[2]

He goes on to note that although skeptics attribute belief in these phenomena to fear of death, such beliefs are also "fueled more cogently by our experiences."[3] These experiences continue to suggest postmortem survival.

Dr. Greyson relates many examples of Peak in Darien experiences, including that of Physician K.M. Dale. Dale told the story of 9-year-old Eddie Cuomo, whose fever finally broke after almost 36 hours. As soon as he opened his eyes, he told his parents that he went to Heaven and spoke of the people he had seen, including his deceased Grandpa Cuomo, Aunt Rosa, and Uncle Lorenzo. But then Eddie shocked those present by saying that he had also seen his 19-year-old sister Teresa, who explained that he had to go back.

Eddie's father became very upset and told his son that he had just spoken to Teresa, who was away at college in Vermont, just two nights before. Later that day, his parents found out that their daughter had indeed been killed in an automobile accident just after midnight.

In addition, Dr. Greyson tells the more recent story of Technicolor pioneer Natalie Kalmus, whose sister Eleanor began calling out the names of deceased loved ones in her final moments. Shortly before Eleanor died, she told those present that her cousin Ruth was there and asked, "What's she doing here?" Ruth had died the week before but Eleanor had not been told.

> I had been hearing and reading about Peak in Darien cases for decades, and considered them among the most convincing, because the role of expectation or wishful thinking in seeing deceased loved ones is minimized when the experiencer does not know the loved one has passed on, or, in some cases, the experiencer had never even known of the existence of the deceased relative. However, I was not aware of any sizable collection of Peak in Darien cases. Frances Cobbe had published a few cases in her 1882 book, but I only occasionally came across more recent examples in various publications throughout the 20th century. I launched a search for Peak in Darien cases in order to create a repository of representative cases and I was surprised to find many detailed examples stretching from ancient Greece and Rome to the present day.

Some of these cases can be quite convincing, for example, when the experiencer describes meeting a deceased person whose death was unknown to anyone else at the time. There are also cases in which the deceased person conveys information to the experiencer that no one living knows, such as the location of a hidden document or treasure. But others, though they are very profound for the experiencer, are less evidential because they have no corroboration from outside sources. These cases can include circumstances in which an experiencer is greeted in an NDE by a loving presence of an unrecognized person and only later identifies that greeter in an old photograph of relatives he or she had not known in this life. Although these cases often convince the experiencer that we live on after death, other people have only the experiencer's testimony that the figure in the photograph was the greeter in the NDE.

Dr. Greyson has been studying near-death phenomena for 40 years and is one of the founding members of the International Association for Near-Death Studies (IANDS). He earned a degree in psychology from Cornell University before going on to receive his medical degree from the State University of New York Upstate Medical College. He is now director emeritus of the division of perceptual studies at the University of Virginia Medical School where he teaches psychiatry and continues to carry out his research.

When asked if there was one that stands out among the various cases he has studied throughout the years, Dr. Greyson noted, "I cannot single out one case among the thousands I have studied. I find a great many to be evidential, but I am also impressed by the cumulative evidential value of the consistency among cases."[4]

No doubt additional research is needed. Dr. Greyson admits that although he has been studying these phenomena for many years, he still doesn't feel like he knows enough. Perhaps this is because the more we know about the unknown, the more we realize just how much there is to know and understand.

Hard-core skeptics will continue to challenge such anecdotal accounts as merely hallucinations and the byproduct of a dying brain. However, these Peak in Darien experiences in which the dying express surprise at seeing a deceased loved one of whose death they had no knowledge is, to many, irrefutable.

"Learning more about our spiritual aspects can help us understand more fully who we are," Dr. Greyson concluded, "and can restore some of the meaning and purpose in life that is harder to appreciate from a purely materialistic perspective of humanity."[5]

For information on Dr. Bruce Greyson, visit *http://archived.para psych.org/members/c_b_greyson.html*. To read "Seeing Dead People Not Known to Have Died: 'Peak in Darien' Experiences," visit: *www.newdualism.org/nde-papers/Greyson/Greyson-Anthropology%20 and%20Humanism_2010-35-159-171.pdf.*

Understanding the Dying Process

Penny Sartori, PhD

Like so many others, Dr. Penny Sartori's research was sparked by a personal experience. An author and renowned researcher in the field of NDEs, she worked for 21 years as a nurse in a British hospital, 17 of which were in intensive care. Dr. Sartori's work has since received worldwide media attention, including that of Prince Charles. In 2005, she was awarded a PhD for her research into NDEs. In talking to Dr. Sartori, she wishes to make one thing clear: Her work is not about investigating whether there is life after death, but rather about understanding the dying process so that care for the terminally ill can be improved.

I couldn't help but wonder what Dr. Sartori's impressive work has taught her about the afterlife. After all, when you study NDEs, you learn without a doubt that life does continue in some form after the spirit leaves the body.

As we've seen previously in this book, witnessing deathbed phenomena is a common occurrence among hospice and palliative care doctors and nurses. Because they work so closely with the dying, they see these experiences first-hand. Dr. Sartori witnessed many as well, but a few stand out among the rest.

My interest in death and NDEs began when I worked as a nurse in the ICU when I was looking after a man who was dying. He was clearly dying, and he knew he was, yet we were doing all we could to keep him alive. He had a very prolonged death and greatly suffered in the end.

I felt as if I'd swapped places with him because I was able to understand what he was going through. I talk about this more extensively in my book *The Wisdom of Near-Death Experiences.* That experience changed everything for me, as it made me realize that we don't actually understand death.

So I was determined to learn more about the dying process so that no other patient had to go through what that man had endured at the end of his life. That was when I came across NDEs.

The primary reason for doing my research was to learn about the dying process so that we can ensure that everyone has as peaceful a transition into death as possible. However, as a result of undertaking my research, it has also raised other important points. One of those points is: We don't understand consciousness. Our current science believes consciousness to be created by the brain, so when a person dies, the brain stops functioning and there is no conscious experience.

Prospective hospital research is showing that patients who had a cardiac arrest have reported a heightened state of consciousness when there should be no experience at all. I think it is therefore important that consciousness is explored from a different aspect: consciousness being mediated through the brain but not created by it. Maybe consciousness is primary, which would have all sorts of implications for our understanding of what it means to be human.

I've witnessed many different deathbed visions that patients were experiencing. When my paternal grandfather was dying we nursed him at home and I remember him pointing to the doorway saying, "Look who is there." This happened many times in the week leading up to his death, and my grandmother would get very upset by this and leave the room. At the time I hadn't begun my research, so I didn't really pay much attention to it.

One experience that sticks in my mind was of a patient who was in my research. He had deteriorated during the night so his family had been called to the ICU in the early hours. They stayed at his bedside for a while and then his condition stabilized so they returned home. Shortly after this my colleague called my attention to the patient because he had become more alert and had started gesturing and talking to someone we couldn't see. He looked really happy and he had a big smile on his face;all of my colleagues commented on how happy he looked.

The next day, his family returned to visit and he told them that he had been visited during the night by his deceased mother and grandmother, but also his sister—he couldn't understand why his sister was with them. Unbeknown to him, his sister had died the week before, but the family did not tell him because they didn't want it to upset him and set back his recovery.

I think ultimately these experiences teach us about life. I'd never looked at it like that when I first became interested in NDEs. When I first started my research, I thought I was going to have all of the answers. Instead what I found was that learning from these people empowered me to live a happy and fulfilled life, which in itself has made me less fearful of death.

What we learn from NDEs can also impact the whole planet in a very positive way. Many people come back with a renewed appreciation for nature and see how we are currently destroying the planet with the destruction of the rain forests, and so on. Consequently, a lot of NDErs adopt eco-friendly behavior.

Dr. Sartori's experience is quite extraordinary and one that I like to call an *evidential deathbed visit* (EDV). In Dr. Sartori's account, the patient did not know that his sister had passed away the week before. This significantly validates the experience. Why would he say that he saw his sister with his deceased mother and grandmother? He had no reason to believe at that point that his sister was deceased.

So, what are NDEs and how do they differ from deathbed visits? The International Association for Near Death Studies (IANDS) defines an NDE as a profound psychological event that may happen to someone who is near death or, if not close to death, is in a situation of physical or emotional crisis.

Some skeptics claim that a near-death experience is merely a vision produced by lack of oxygen to the brain (cerebral hypoxia), or even hallucinations brought on by drugs. Typically, we can live for about seven minutes without oxygen. Yet many who have reported having a near-death experience were without oxygen for far more than seven minutes.

Dr. Melvin Morse, author and NDE researcher, once told me a story about a girl who drowned in a swimming pool and was without oxygen for 20 minutes. Not only did she survive, but she also fully recovered and told him details about what took place during her resuscitation. She explained how she went through a tunnel to a beautiful place she believed to be Heaven. She then told Dr. Morse, who was then a skeptic, "Don't worry, Dr. Morse. Heaven is fun."[1]

And as for the theory that NDEs are hallucinatory and brought on by drugs, Dr. Morse studied 26 children who came close to death and compared them to 131 others who were treated with drugs such as morphine. He found that 23 out of the 26 children who nearly died reported having an NDE while none of the other 131 children had them.[2]

Although scientists may consider these studies to be circumstantial evidence, the data strongly implies that consciousness survives death, and that there is in fact life after death. For example:

- Aspects of quantum physics support NDE concepts, including the properties of light, non-locality, and multi-dimensional reality, to name a few. Light is a common link among most NDEs.
- People who are blind can see during a near-death experience.
- Many NDErs experienced out of body experiences (OBEs) while unconscious and were able to later accurately describe what took place.
- NDErs have returned with accurate knowledge about future events.

Dr. Sartori explained these experiences in more detail.

NDEs are an acute experience of dying as opposed to deathbed visions, which tend to occur over a period of weeks/days leading up to the time of death. Some people who have recovered from a close brush with death, whether through an accident, near drowning, critical illness, or cardiac arrest have reported a transcendent experience. They may feel like they leave their body and look down on the emergency situation from above, they may travel through darkness toward a very bright light, then find themselves in a beautiful place with lovely scenery such as lush green grass and vividly colored flowers. Some people meet deceased relatives or a being of light who telepathically tell them it is not their time and that they have to return. Some people have a life review where they relive their life in great detail and in many cases can feel the impact that their actions have had on others. When these people return to life they are usually profoundly transformed in many ways including spiritually, physically, and psychologically.

As noted earlier, it was an experience with a dying patient that led Dr. Sartori to study these spiritual phenomena. In fact, her experience upset her so much that she considered giving up nursing. Luckily, however, she decided to take a different route and instead read every book about death that she could find. Her intent was to understand the dying process so that care for the terminally ill could be improved. She shared her thoughts on why such research is so important and how it has changed her personally.

It has certainly made me more open-minded. I was very skeptical of these experiences when I first heard of them because of the preconceptions that I'd grown up with. Having undertaken my research I realize that there was no evidential basis for those preconceptions; they were just explanations that I'd accepted without even exploring them further.

Doing my research has also made me think about, and live, my life very differently and I feel much more empowered and fulfilled as a result. It is only when we begin to learn about death that we really begin to learn about life.

It is crucial that we study all of these phenomena because they give us insights into the dying process and can therefore guide us when caring for people at the end of their life. By acknowledging NDEs and deathbed visits we can validate these experiences for those who have them. Unfortunately the spiritual needs of patients often get overlooked, and by fully addressing the spiritual needs of the dying person, we can then help them have a peaceful transition into death.

I think these experiences can also be helpful and beneficial for those who are grieving the loss of a loved one. Very frequently people mention to me little signs or coincidences that they noticed after the death of a loved one. Sometimes these signs can be so subtle that they can be easily missed. If more people were more aware of the possibility of such signs or communications it may help greatly with their grieving process.

These are all essential parts of the human experience and they should be in everyone's education from a young age. Deathbed scenes years ago were a social event; the whole community visited the dying person in their home and this included children. People were more prepared and therefore more accepting of death. Children grew up with an awareness of death and they weren't sheltered from it. Nowadays death has been relegated to a lonely room in a hospital where the dying person feels very much alienated from those around them.

As noted various times in this book, many who have these transformative experiences say that, as a result, they have no fear of death. And as Dr. Sartori noted, they also point out that understanding what awaits them on the Other Side has helped them to live a happier, more fulfilling life.

There is such great insight and wisdom in what people have to say following an NDE. They teach us that we are all one and all interconnected; basically what we do to others comes back on ourselves. This is the Golden Rule: "Do unto others as you would wish done unto yourself," which is at the heart of all the great wisdom traditions. If we all lived by that rule how different our world would be.

Like Dr. Sartori, I hoped to have most if not all the answers, but as I delved further into my research, I came to realize that there is still so much we as a society don't understand. Some things we will come to know in due time. Some things, however, we will never know until we ourselves cross over.

> I think that people's attitudes toward NDEs and other death-bed phenomena have greatly changed since I first began researching them in 1996. Initially I found it very hard to find people who would share their NDE with me. As time progressed I found more and more people but they were still very hesitant and cautious. I began to build up a database and then a newspaper article was published about my hospital research around 2006 and I received hundreds of emails in response to that from people who wanted to share their NDE with me. Last year my book came out and in the first few months I was receiving about 200 emails a day, which have gradually reduced to about 200 a week, mainly from people who want to share their experiences. This is a huge contrast to when I first started out.

> People now feel more comfortable with sharing their experience because more people are aware of them. Before there were a lot of very cynical attitudes from people who had never had an NDE or witnessed any deathbed phenomena, but those attitudes are changing. It's so encouraging to see people open their minds to a greater understanding of these important experiences because let's face it: They are of importance to each and every one of us. We are all going to die and I

feel a lot more prepared for my own death having undertaken my research.

We may not have all the answers, but we have undoubtedly come a long way. More and more people are coming forward and sharing their experiences. I am confident that we will someday go back to treating death as an essential part of life rather give it the taboo treatment. The way we view mortality has already changed for the better. Deathbed visits, near-death experiences, afterlife communication, and other spiritual phenomena are at the forefront of this change.

When asked if there was just one message she hoped to convey through both her research and her books, Dr. Sartori said, "Let the message of the NDE empower your life and do not be afraid of death nor life. Live life to the fullest and enjoy it for the gift it is."

Very wise words from a very wise woman.

For more information about Dr. Penny Sartori, visit *www.drpenny sartori.com.*

 ## Shankar

Ramya, India, www.meotherwise.com

Just a month back, I had met with my father's oncologist. "The cancer is terminal," she said. I asked with a grim face, "So how long?" A tough question for any doctor to answer, but she answered, diplomatically, "Months, maybe weeks." I got the message. My father wasn't going to make it.

His first sign of impending death came sooner than expected. The onset of jaundice in terminal liver cancer marks the beginning of the end. The liver is a vital organ responsible for regulating metabolic activities across our bodies. A failure would mean a slow death of all other vital organs. The unregulated count of ammonia in the blood becomes a toxin to the brain. This eventually leads to hepatic coma.

My dad lay on his deathbed, mumbling and moaning. I noticed his eyes—they were transfixed on the door. The door was not directly in front of him;he had to tilt his head to the right in order to see it, so his staring was very obvious. What amazed me was the fact that his speech was very clear and coherent. He began calling out "Amma! Amma!" He was speaking in Tamil—our mother tongue. He called out, "Mother, you have finally come? Where had you been?" An hour or so passed and he then called out again, "Shankar, you have come, too. And you look so young." Shankar was my mother's brother, whom my father had always disliked.

Upon hearing this last line, I instantly felt a sudden chill. I realized that my father was having deathbed visions. He was talking to my grandmother and uncle—both deceased. When my father began calling out to his mother, I thought perhaps it was because he was in pain. Don't we all cry out to our moms when we are in pain? But when he called out to my Uncle Shankar, I was taken aback.

I even went to see his oncologist to ask her about my father's chattering. She told me that the power of the brain is such that we really have no answers. She also noted that it was common for people with excess ammonia in their blood to hallucinate. But when I asked her about the clarity in my father's voice, the doctor said it was probably just my imagination due to my emotional state at that time. Her answers didn't convince me, and I didn't agree with her. There was something in his eyes when he stared at the door; I knew there was much more to it.

Witnessing these deathbed visits was new to me. I was watching someone die right in front of me for the first time. At first, I didn't know what it was and felt very confused. My mom explained that per Indian traditions, when a person begins to call out to the deceased, it means their time is nearing. In scientific literature such experiences have been referred to as death-related sensory experiences (DRSE). Many dying patients have often reported such visions of comfort to hospice staff around them. The scientific community considers deathbed phenomena and visions to be hallucinations.

Specific studies on deathbed phenomena have described the visual, auditory, and sensed presences of deceased relatives or angelic beings during the dying process as hallucinations. These hallucinations, they often say, occur due to cerebral hypoxia. When the body is injured, or if the heart stops, even if only for a short period, the brain is deprived of oxygen. A short period of cerebral hypoxia can result in the impairment of neural function.

I have almost always looked up to science for life's various questions and mysteries. Yet, for what I have experienced watching my dad dying, I still haven't received any convincing answers. The hallucination theory still leaves many questions unanswered.

Why were there only dead people in my father's so-called hallucinations? If this was a game of the brain, why did he call out to an uncle whom he seldom liked? How come he had such clarity in his voice? He wasn't coherent and responsive otherwise. He seemed to be in a trance much of the time and wasn't able to communicate. Yet, when he had these deathbed visions, he was able to speak clearly.

As I sat at Dad's bedside during his last few hours, I was greatly comforted in many ways by these deathbed visions. Despite his pain, the thought of family members waiting to take him was reassuring. Having them there certainly made his transition from this world to the beyond much easier. Hopefully, as time goes by, science will finally be able to give us greater insight into such deathbed phenomena.

 ## I Keep Seeing People

Judy, New Jersey

My husband, John, had been sick with a cold. He worked in retail management but he took off to rest at home. It was a Wednesday afternoon, and I called him to see how he was feeling and to ask if he needed me to pick up anything for him on my way home from work.

I can't say I was prepared for his response. John was sitting at the dining room table at the time and told me bluntly, "I'm sitting here writing the bills and I keep seeing people running around the dining room table. I think they're all dead people."

I honestly thought all the cough medicine he had been taking for his cold symptoms was making him hallucinate and imagine things. "John," I told him, "stop taking that crazy cough medicine!" His doctor had also just started him on a prescription for his chronic obstructive pulmonary disease (COPD). So, again, I thought perhaps the combination of all these medications was making him imagine things. I honestly didn't think much of it at the time.

On the way home, I stopped to pick up a couple of ice-cream sundaes. John and I ate them at the dining room table that night and we later went to bed about 10 o'clock.

Later that night I was awakened by what sounded like a loud thud. I didn't know what it was, so I quickly rushed to see what happened. I found my husband on the floor in the dining room. He had been sitting at the table when he had a massive heart attack and fell off the chair.

My husband was not able to be resuscitated and passed away. John would sometimes get up in the middle of the night and drive to Dunkin Donuts for coffee. He had been coughing and not feeling well and had done just that. On the table were two unopened cups of coffee.

The next morning I discovered that my car was damaged on one side. The car was scratched as if he had swiped against something on his way home. I can only think that this was the onset of his heart attack.

When I think back to that day, I now realize that John was not hallucinating. John did believe in an afterlife and definitely had faith in the unseen. I don't know who those spirits were, but it's comforting to know my husband was not alone.

A Soul Departing?

Marisa, NE Texas

I have over 20 years of experience as an ICU/trauma nurse. An experience I shall never forget occurred over 15 years ago in a step-down unit. I was working the night shift in the ICU as team leader; the step-down unit was next to our unit. Around 0200 a young nurse from the step-down unit came over and asked me to check on a patient whose eyes were open but who was not responding to verbal or noxious stimuli.

When I saw the patient, it became evident a code blue (cardiac arrest) had to be started right away. That night we were short on IV poles, so I played the role of IV pole, holding up the bags of fluids and overseeing the code. Later, one of the respiratory therapists took over the IV pole role and I went to sit on the chair. I had a really good view of the patient.

Suddenly I saw something that amazed me. From the patient's chest area I saw something rise into the air. The best way I can describe it is that it looked like that shimmering one sees rising over the highway on a very hot summer day. If I had to give it a color I would say it was mainly silver and had an occasional sparkle to it. It appeared to be contained, nearly oval in shape, but I lost sight of it when it reached about 3 feet above the patient.

At the same time, something inside told me that the patient was not coming back—and she did not. She was only 52 years old and, as we sometimes say in the medical field, had no reason to take such a turn.

Will I Go to Heaven?

This story is reprinted with permission from www.ghostsn
ghouls.com.

A young woman had full liver failure. She was orange in color and she was still conscious. She asked me what I thought it would be like to die. I told her I didn't know, but that I hoped it wouldn't be painful. She then asked me if I thought I would go to Heaven. I told her that I believed I would. She asked me if I thought she would go to Heaven, and I told her I wasn't able to answer that question.

She then told me, "I am going to Heaven and I know it." I asked her how she knew that and she told me something that I will never ever forget: "I know I am because that man over there told me so." I asked what man and she said the man sitting on the end of the bench. I asked her what he looked like and she said, "He looks just like the Jesus on the windows of my church."

Well, I was pretty affected by that statement. She then went on to say, "And he says that you are going to go to Heaven, too." We then prayed and I will never forget that interaction between the two of us. About a week later she passed away. I hope she made it to Heaven.

Life's Mysteries Are Revealed in Its Final Moments

Dr. Michael Barbato

In the 1600s, Galileo Galilei (1564–1642) was charged with heresy and forced into house arrest by the Catholic Church simply because his advanced beliefs were not supported by the masses. At that time, just about everyone thought the Earth was the center of the universe. They also believed that the Earth was flat. So when Galileo, an Italian astronomer, mathematician, and physicist said otherwise, people thought he was crazy. Only he wasn't crazy at all; he was right.

Galileo was not alone; many of the world's greatest minds were ridiculed and laughed out of the lab only to be later vindicated. This is nothing new. Whenever anyone proposes a different way of thinking or a new paradigm that goes against or threatens our preconceived notions of reality, most of us are quick to reject it. But as Albert

Einstein cleverly noted, "What is right is not always popular and what is popular is not always right."

When Dr. Michael Barbato first began writing about spiritual phenomena such as deathbed visits in the late 1990s, many people thought he was fanciful and his ideas were far-fetched. Times have changed, however. Today, he's a sought-after speaker addressing doctors, nurses, and palliative care professionals around the country. His way of thinking is no longer thought of as weird and imaginary. Nowadays, he says, people come prepared to listen.

Now retired, Dr. Barbato was in a medical practice for more than 50 years, with more than 25 devoted to palliative care. "The move into palliative care was precipitated by the death of our newborn child some years earlier," he said. "This devastating event led my wife, Ann, and I to re-examine our lives, our priorities, and our values."[1]

In addition to his child's death, an unforgettable experience with a patient named Ian finally convinced him to make the move. Ian, a young man dying of acute leukemia, had lapsed into a coma. Although he was expected to die within 24 hours, he defied all odds and held on for several days, awakening—to the amazement of everyone in the room—just as his sister arrived from overseas.

> To have someone survive for as long as he did and then awake from his unconscious state just as his sister walked into the room (after travelling from the USA) was beyond belief and did not fit in with my medical understanding of unconsciousness. Ian died very shortly after his sister's arrival and this suggested that, on some level, he was aware and had chosen to remain alive until she arrived.
>
> Since then I have had the privilege of witnessing and hearing numerous stories that have a mystical quality about them. One of the more memorable involved an elderly Italian woman who was dying of cancer. She had been admitted to the palliative care ward, but the family asked us not to tell her that she had cancer and was dying. We reluctantly abided

by their wish and colluded with this loving lie until one day when the woman became uncharacteristically animated and appeared to be looking at something. In her native tongue, she excitedly called out, "My boat has come, my bags are packed, I am going on a beautiful holiday, and none of you can come with me." The family thought she was delirious and asked that she be sedated. When told this was a deathbed vision and that their mother was simply saying that she knew she was dying and was not afraid, the family for the first time told their mother how much they loved her and would miss her. This was a conversation they would not have had without that deathbed vision.[2]

Dr. Barbato wholeheartedly disputes the idea that these visions are hallucinations caused by morphine or the byproduct of a dying brain. In his book, *Reflections of a Setting Sun,* he tells of a patient who claimed to see spiders and strange creatures. At the same time, the patient also reported visions of his deceased brother. The patient was on morphine at the time. Once the morphine was substituted with another drug, Dr. Barbato noted that the spider hallucinations stopped. The visions of his deceased brother, however, continued until he took his last breath.

Working for so many years with the dying, their journeys, and the many experiences he witnessed taught him as much about life as they did about death.

Working with the dying has taught me that the best preparation for death is to lead a full and self-actualizing life. I also believe it is necessary to have an inner life that balances and sustains me in the world that I live and work in. The better a person I become, the more present I can be for those that I love and care for.

The most valuable lessons that I have learned are to live in the moment and to realize that my greatest contribution to patient care is not what I do for them, but how I can be there for them. This is difficult for someone trained to make people better and so I now attempt to marry the science of care with the art of caring. These two models of care are complementary and, not as many would think, mutually exclusive.[3]

In his book, *Reflections of a Setting Sun*, he writes, "Dying, more than any other life event, presents us with the opportunity to grow, to change, to love, to appreciate and ultimately to experience the meaning of our existence. Our death is the completion of our life's mission. The setting sun may have lost much of its early brightness but this has unexpected rewards for it can, often for the first time, be clearly seen. It seems paradoxical, but truth and the mystery of 'Who am I?' are often revealed in the final moments of our life."[4]

The purpose in writing his books, he is quick to point out, is not to prove the existence of an afterlife, but rather to stress the need for a more holistic approach to end-of-life care. He writes that death is not simply the end of life. Rather, it is a profound human experience.

As someone approaches death, their emotional and spiritual needs are as great if not greater than those of their body. If we attend only to the physical envelope, the soul suffers and the real significance of death is lost, as is the opportunity for sharing and healing. Deathbed visions and other near-to-death experiences are part of this healing process. They are extraordinary gifts waiting to be shared but often remain unseen and unopened if hidden by the trappings of medical care.[5]

When people are dying, Barbato considers love and fear to be the most common and powerful emotions that occupy the mind. The dying will fear leaving their loved ones and any pain they may have to endure before they die. However, it is the love they give and receive that sustains them and gives them the courage to go forward. The more we prepare for death, the easier the transition.

Those who do not prepare are not ready (psych-spiritually) for death when it comes. Death, for them, is often painful, emotional, and seen as a tragedy rather than the natural end to life. So, the best way to prepare for death (apart from all the practical things such as having a living will, advance care directive, etc.) is to live life fully, and to have a spiritual or inner reflective life. It's also important to be grateful for all that we have in this life and to listen to our innate wisdom and that of others.[6]

Dr. Barbato has witnessed and has had many patients share their deathbed visits with him. So many, in fact, that it is impossible for him to note which one touched him the most. Although he won't single one out, he did say that witnessing such experiences has made him aware of how much they help the dying. "Those that have a vision or a profound dream often say they no longer fear death and, from his experience they die in a state of equanimity that has to be seen to be believed."[7]

Having retired from his medical practice in 2012, he now conducts courses on death and dying and is engaged in research for end-of-life care in his native Australia. "What I hope to achieve is to awaken people to the need to live life fully and to mend broken bridges before it is too late," he said. "I also hope to alert people to the fact that life is a precious gift that must be returned at some unknown time in the future (hopefully, not unopened)."[8]

For more information on Dr. Michael Barbato, visit *www.caring forthedying.iinet.net.au.*

Mistakes Are Made in Love's Service

Dr. Joan Borysenko

My mother was a formidable woman. This story is her legacy, and a lesson about the spiritual art of forgiveness. Whenever I tell it, deep gratitude for the gift of her life takes me by surprise, as if I'm experiencing her soul face to face for the very first time. Part of the magic of the forgiveness we shared together is that it's always new for me, no matter how many times I tell her story. In that newness, a bit of grace often gets transmitted to those who hear or read it.

The morning of her death, in the late 1980s, my mother was transported to the basement of the hospital where I worked. She was bleeding internally, and they'd sent her down to radiology to get a fix on the source. She was gone for hours. My worried family, who had gathered in her room to say good-bye, finally sent me to search for her. I found her alone, lying on a gurney, in the hospital corridor. She'd been waiting her turn for an x-ray there, with nothing but the bare walls as a companion for several hours.

I found the doctor in charge and asked if I could take her back to her room. He shook his head from side to side, frowning. "I'm sorry, but she's bleeding," he said. "We need a diagnosis."

My mother, as pale as the sheet she was lying on, colored up a little and raised an eyebrow. "A diagnosis? Is that all you need? You mean to tell me that I've been lying here all day just because you needed a diagnosis? Why didn't you ask me?"

The doctor, who looked as if he'd just seen a ghost, was speechless for a bit. He finally stammered out a weak, "Wh-wh-what do you mean?"

"I'm dying; that's your diagnosis," my mother replied with her usual humor. To his credit, the doctor saw her point, and I was able to talk him into letting me take her back to her room. We were supposed to wait for an orderly to do the transport, but she begged me to go AWOL and speed her back to the family before anyone else could grab her. We were finally alone together in the elevator, riding back up to her floor. She looked up at me from the gurney, transparent in the way that small children and elderly people often are. There was no artifice—she was who she was. She reached for my hand, looked into my eyes, and said very simply that she'd made a lot of mistakes as a mother, and asked if I could forgive her. The pain of a lifetime evaporated in that brief journey between floors.

I kissed her hand and then her clammy cheek. "Of course I forgive you," I whispered through a throat swollen with tears. "Can you forgive me for all the times I've judged you, for all the times I wasn't there for you? I've made a lot of mistakes as a daughter, too." She smiled and nodded at me as tears welled up in her rheumy eyes, once a striking cobalt blue more beautiful than the sky. Love built a bridge across a lifetime of guilt, hurt, and shame.

When we returned to her room, each family member had a few minutes alone with her to say good-bye. Then, as day disappeared into long shadows, and the early spring night fell like a curtain around us, everyone left except my brother, Alan; my son, Justin; and me. We three were the vigil keepers.

Justin was a young man of 20 and fiercely devoted to the grandmother who had always been his champion. He seemed to know intuitively what a dying person needs to hear—that her life had meaning, and that she had left the world a little bit better off by her presence. He told her stories of their good times together, of how her love had sustained him. Justin held his dying grandmother in his arms, sang to her, prayed for her, and read to her for much of her last night with us. I was so proud of him.

Unusual things can happen at births and deaths. The veil between this world and the next is thin at these gateways, as souls enter and leave. Around midnight, Mom fell into a final morphine-assisted sleep. Justin and I were alone with her while my brother took a break. We were meditating on either side of her bed, but I was awake, not asleep; I was perfectly lucid, not dreaming. The world seemed to shift on its axis, and I had a vision, which if you've ever had one, you know seems realer than real. This life appears to be the dream, and the vision a glimpse of a deeper reality.

In the vision, I was a pregnant mother, laboring to give birth. I was also the baby being born. It was an odd, yet deeply familiar experience

to be one consciousness present in two bodies. With a sense of pene-
trating insight and certainty, I realized that there's only one consciousness in the entire universe. Despite the illusion of separateness, there's
only one of us here, and that One is the Divine.

As the baby moved down the birth canal, my consciousness
switched entirely into its tiny body. I felt myself moving down the dark
tunnel. It was frightening, a death of sorts, as I left the watery darkness
of the womb to travel through this unknown territory. I emerged quite
suddenly into a place of perfect peace, complete comfort, and ineffable
Light—the sort that people tell about in near-death experiences.

The Light is beyond any kind of description. No words can express
the total love, absolute forgiveness, tender mercy, Divine bliss, complete reverence, awesome holiness, and eternal peace that the Light
is. That Light of Divine love seemed to penetrate my soul. I felt as
though it had seen and known my every thought, motive, action, and
emotion in this life. In spite of my obvious shortcomings and terrible
errors, it held me in absolute gentleness, complete forgiveness, and
unconditional love as you would a small child. I knew beyond question, cradled in the Light, that love is who we are and what we are
becoming.

Scenes of my mother and me together flashed by. Many of these
scenes were of difficult times when our hearts were closed to one
another and we were not in our best selves. Yet, from the vantage point
of the Light, every interaction seemed perfect, calculated to teach us
something about loving better. As the scenes went on, life's mysterious
circularity came clear. Mom had birthed me into this world, and I had
birthed her soul back out. We were one. I was reborn at the moment
of her death—bathed in love, forgiveness, and gratitude. I thought
of the words of St. Paul, that we see through a glass, darkly. For a
moment I was granted the gift of seeing face to face.

When I opened my eyes, the entire room was bathed in light.
Peace was like a palpable presence, a velvety stillness, the essence of
Being. All things appeared to be interconnected, without boundaries.

I remembered how my high school chemistry teacher had explained that everything was made of energy, of light. That night I could see it. Everything was part of a whole, pulsing with the Light of Creation. I looked across my mother's dead body and saw my son sitting opposite me. Justin's face was luminous. It looked as though he had a halo. He was weeping softly, tears like diamonds glinting with light. I got up and walked around the bed, pulling a chair up close to him. He looked deep into my eyes and asked softly whether I could see that the room was filled with light. I nodded, and we held hands in the silence. After a few beats, he whispered reverently that the Light was his grandma's last gift. "She's holding open the door to eternity so that we can have a glimpse," he told me.

Continuing to look deeply into my eyes, Justin spoke from a well of wisdom deeper than his 20 years. "You must be so grateful to your mother," he said. I knew exactly what he meant. I'd been an ungrateful daughter, holding on to years of grudges against my difficult mom. Now my heart was overflowing with gratitude, which was a completely new emotion with respect to her.

It turned out that Justin had also had a vision, which to this day he has kept to himself. But he told me these things there in the hospital room where the shell of his beloved grandmother's 81-year-old body lay. My mother, he said, was a great soul, a wise being who had far more wisdom than her role in this lifetime had allowed her to express. She had taken a role much smaller than who she was, he assured me, so that I would have someone to resist. In resisting her, I would have to become myself. My purpose in life, he explained—a purpose in which she had played a vital part—was to share the gift of what I'd learned about healing, compassion, God, and self-discovery.

I looked down at the floor to gather myself, and then back into my son's gentle green eyes. "Can you forgive me, Justin? I know I've made a lot of mistakes as a mother. Do you know how much I love you?"

He took my hand. "Mistakes are made in love's service," he whispered. And then the energy in the room shifted, the Light faded, and we hugged for a long time. Finally breaking away, he smiled and laughed, "Hey, Mom, you wounded me in just the right ways."

We got up and did a silly little dance together that we saw Ren and Stimpy, the cartoon characters, do one day on television. "Happy Happy, Joy Joy!" we chanted as we danced around incongruously in the room of a dead mother, a dead grandmother, whose love we had shared and experienced in very different ways.

"Please remember that you forgive me, sweetheart," I reminded Justin a little while later. "I'm sure that I'm not done making mistakes yet."

In the 20-plus years since we shared my mother's death, Justin and I have both made mistakes, and we've both taken responsibility for them and made amends as best we could. But the grace of mother-child forgiveness, and the sense that we're here together because we're learning to love, has made the process much easier. For that alone, I'm so very grateful.

Dr. Joan Borysenko is a world-renowned expert in the mind/body connection. Her work has been foundational in an international health-care revolution that recognizes the role of meaning and the spiritual dimensions of life as an integral part of health and healing. As a psychologist, she was appointed instructor in medicine at the Harvard Medical School, where she also earned her doctorate in medical sciences. Her years of clinical experience and research culminated in the publication of the *New York Times* best-seller *Minding the Body, Mending the Mind*, which sold more than 400,000 copies. She has authored or coauthored several other books and is a popular speaker. For more information, visit *www.joanborysenko.com/*.

A Patient Named John Loranger

Barbara Harris Whitfield, United States

Having had two near-death experiences a week apart from each other in 1975, Barbara Harris Whitfield is no stranger to spiritual phenomena. She spent six years researching the after-effects of the NDE with Bruce Greyson, MD, at the University of Connecticut Medical School. While there, Whitfield was called in to work with a patient named John Loranger, whom she will never forget.

I witnessed John's death after getting to know him for about six weeks. In his early 30s, he was paralyzed and completely bed-ridden, dependent on the staff to take care of his every need. His only movement came from his ability to speak, and he was quickly losing that too. At the very end, he was dependent on an electronic voice box placed on his throat that didn't help the confusion of what he was trying to say.

John fought through his lawyers and friends to be disconnected from life support. This was in the 1980s, and John became the first patient to die by being disconnected from life support in Connecticut. I was a witness to that process. When he was disconnected at about 10 a.m., one of John's last statements through the voice box was, "They are coming for me at 5 o'clock." No one understood what he said, so I repeated his words, saying, "He says, 'They are coming for me at 5 o'clock.'"

John was given an injection with a sedative and respiratory depressant and went into a peaceful sleep. At 10:10 a.m. he was disconnected from the machinery that kept him alive, but he didn't die right away. He died at exactly 5 o'clock.

The staff showed all the signs of mourning for John because he had been there for several weeks, and they all knew him and cared for him. But because of the unpredictable way of dying many hours after the life support was removed, and his announcement of when he was to actually die, many staff, including the physicians, acted out in negative ways. What I mostly heard from them was pain over not being able to control the way John's death happened, thinking perhaps they botched the procedure, and pain over not being able to save his life, plus some unresolved issues that people express when they feel helpless in the face of death.

Making the transition from this world is so much bigger than any other ritual on this planet. Souls come in. Souls go out. Birth is a joyous event. Death is beyond our comprehension. We live in a material reality that limits our ability to experience the sacred and celebratory side of death: the final passage from this reality to a nonphysical and eternal one.

Helping someone die is as close as I can get, as close as any of us can get, to the huge reality that is beyond our individual ability to perceive. Ultimately, all of this is a mystery, but we can get closer to the mystery by allowing ourselves to experience death with openness, loss of ego, and willingness to be aware of and open to our subtle experience.

———

Barbara Harris Whitfield is a researcher, therapist, and author of several books. She presents workshops on near-death experiences, thanatology (the study of death and dying), and spirituality. For more information, visit *www.barbara-whitfield.com.*

I Will See You at 9 O'clock

Patricia Lazaro, New York

When my husband, Joe, was sick and dying, I felt as though I was dying, too. It almost felt like I had each of my feet in two different worlds—one foot on the Other Side and one here on this Earth. At that time, I received many signs from Spirit that still continue to comfort me to this day.

One night, I went to bed before Joe and was alone in the bedroom—or so I thought. I soon felt that I was not alone and sensed a spiritual presence. I am very in tune to the spirit realm and whenever deceased loved ones are around I get a tingling sensation all over. The same thing happened on this particular night and I instinctively knew it was someone I missed very much because I started to sob, saying out loud, "I miss you so much." Suddenly, I heard a voice clearly say, "You will be coming soon."

My spirit or soul knew who it was but I did not. A feeling of love and peace embraced me at that moment. I was also told that Joe would be coming soon but I had to stay here a while longer as my work wasn't done. The voice also told me, "I will see you at 9 o'clock." I had no idea what was meant by this at the time. Why was I being told 9 o'clock?

This experience took place about one year before Joe passed. There is no time on the Other Side as we know it here on Earth. So saying, "Joe would be coming soon," can be a long time to us. As I said, in Joe's case, it was about a year.

During that same year before Joe passed, I had a beautiful dream in which God's arm shot through the other realm to me. God put his arm around me and I felt this vast, unspeakable love. There are no words to describe it.

As I think back to that time before my husband's death, I believe Spirit was consoling me, letting me know what awaited Joe. It was God's way of helping me to deal with losing him, and it does help so very much.

When we are married under God, we are considered one, and I think that is why I experienced all of that. Joe and I shared a very special, deep love and still do. That love will never die.

On the night that my husband passed away, I was home resting when I sensed a strong presence in the room. I got chills all through my body. I quickly grabbed the phone to call the hospital, glancing over at the clock as I did. The time was exactly 9 p.m. The hospital staff informed me that Joe had just taken a turn for the worse and advised that I come right away.

He passed away before I arrived. As I walked into Joe's room in the intensive care unit, I had a vision of many angels wrapping their wings around him to take his soul to Heaven. The vision was over in an instant, but I knew this was Joe sharing his crossing with me. I walked over to him, knowing that he was no longer in his body, and sobbed uncontrollably. Over the years, several psychic mediums have told me that Joe came right to me when he passed.

I have always been a firm believer in God and the afterlife. Joe was a strong believer as well. Not surprisingly, I have received several signs from Joe since he passed. As Saint Augustine once said, "Faith is to believe what you do not see; the reward of this faith is to see what you believe." Joe received his reward and someday I will receive mine.

The Angel of Death

Lisa M., Pennsylvania

I was working a night shift and had gone back to our staff room to get something. On the way back to the nurse's station, I was checking the rooms as I walked by, which was something I always did. As I walked past the second room down the hall, I quickly noticed a dark, human-shaped figure at the foot of the bed. Honestly, I didn't think too much off it initially. I actually passed the room and then realized that the patient in that room was too ill to be out of bed. So at this point, I quickly backed up and looked back in the room but there was nothing there. The patient, an older man with prostate cancer, was actually in bed with the covers over him and he appeared to be sleeping.

When I got to the nurse's station, I was a bit unnerved and sat down with the other nurses. One LPN named Darlene, who had worked as a nurse for many years, noticed the look on my face and asked me what was wrong. I explained what I had just seen in the room. Darlene, however, surprised me when she stated, matter-of-factly, "Oh, you probably just saw the Angel of Death." It didn't appear to faze Darlene at all. It seemed to me like she was quite used to these experiences.

At that point, the RN whose patient it was went racing back to see if he was okay, which I had already checked, and he was still with us. The next day, however, he passed away.

Looking back, I wasn't afraid by the experience, just bemused. I didn't get any bad vibes from the figure, but I didn't get good vibes either. It was unthreatening but hard to explain in many ways. Twenty-five years have passed since that experience. You see a lot as a nurse, but that experience stuck with me.

As nurses, many of us hate it when a patient says a family member or a friend was just here and we find out that the person they are referring to is actually deceased. We know this more often than not means that the patient will soon code or pass away.

In another case, I was with a coworker and we were cleaning up a patient. Suddenly, I felt a cool breeze and could sense someone or something behind me. There was no one there and I told the other nurse that I was pretty sure this patient was going to cross over soon. It totally freaked her out but I ended up being right. A few days later, when I returned to work, I found out that the patient did indeed pass away.

To be honest, I'm caught between being a skeptic and believing. Nurses talk about strange things happening all the time, but most of us are pretty cold, hard realists. In the play *Hamlet* by William Shakespeare, Hamlet says to Horatio, "There are more things in Heaven and earth, Horatio, than are dreamt of in your philosophy." This is said to mean that neither scientists, skeptics, nor even the most highly educated can be surer of the truth than anyone else.

This may be true. But as George Washington once said, "Truth will ultimately prevail where there is pains to bring it to light."

Prophetic Dreaming

Shelley E. Parker

We were newlyweds with big dreams and high hopes for a bright future. So when we were trying to start a family and my husband, John, was offered a job with Cantor Fitzgerald, a brokerage firm in New York City, it was music to my ears. He had two opportunities on the table. The other was with a rival brokerage firm but it was not a management-level position like the other and the pay was less.

In my mind, the choice was an easy one. In fact, there was no contest. The only problem was my husband, for one reason or another, didn't agree. John had a strong feeling that he shouldn't take the job with Cantor Fitzgerald and he had no idea why. He would be reporting to a friend and former boss, Rich Lee, whom he admired greatly. Although he wanted to once again work for Rich, his gut was telling him otherwise.

John and I argued over his decision, as I thought he'd be crazy to pass up an upper management–level position. I honestly thought my husband had lost his senses.

On September 11, 2001, all of Cantor Fitzgerald's 658 employees who reported to work on the 105th floor of One World Trade Center were killed—including Rich Lee. Had my husband listened to me, I would have been widowed.

Our sixth sense is our ability to perceive the unseen world or another dimension. This includes everything from extra-sensory perception (ESP), clairvoyance, telepathy, premonitions, and so on. We perceive our earthly or seen world through the five senses (taste, sound, sight, touch, and smell). But we perceive the unseen through our intuition or our connection to Spirit.

Premonitions are basically forewarnings or gut feelings of what is about to happen. More often, premonitions occur in the form of a dream (also known as prophetic dreams) while we are asleep. I woke up one Saturday morning feeling very anxious because I had a dream that I just couldn't get out of my mind. In the dream, I was at my friend Christina's house standing in her hallway and there were a lot of people around me. Suddenly, I heard Christina calling my name. "Josie! Josie!" I looked up and saw her heading up the stairs to the second floor. She stopped, turned to face me, and said, "I fell. I fell."

At this point, I noticed that her left knee was bleeding badly. I tried to get to Christina, but there were people ahead of me on the stairs and I became very frustrated. When I finally got to the top of the steps, I wasn't in my friend's house at all, but in what looked like a very large room with people everywhere. I looked around but couldn't find my friend. I then went up to at least two people and said, "Where is Chris?" to which they replied, "She's right over there." Yet again, I looked for her and couldn't find her. There also seemed to be this foggy mist in the room. The dream ended with me still searching for my friend.

Christina is one of my closest friends; premonitions often involve people that we have a deep connection with or love. I called that day and told her about the dream. She told me that she was going to a party that evening. I then told her to be careful because I was concerned about the dream. I just couldn't shake off the feeling that the dream was some kind of a message.

Naturally I was worried, but Saturday night came and went without incident. On Monday, I called my friend, and from the way she answered the phone, I could tell that she was in pain. When I asked her what was wrong, she replied, "I fell." I thought for sure I must have misunderstood her and asked, "What did you say?" She then repeated herself (forgetting about the dream), "I fell."

I was stunned and replied, "You fell?! And did you happen to hurt your knee?!" At this point, it hit her and she said, "OH MY GOD! Yes! I hurt my knee and it's bleeding like crazy!" I then asked her which knee she injured. Her response: "My left knee."

Although not all prophetic dreams are negative, most are warnings of what is about to happen. In his book, *The Power of Premonitions:*

How Knowing the Future Can Shape Our Lives, Larry Dossey, MD, tells the story of a woman who dreamed that a chandelier on the ceiling fell and crushed her baby. She also noticed, in the dream, that the clock read 4:35. She woke up, obviously upset about her dream, and decided to go get the baby and bring the baby back to bed with her. Moments later, she heard a loud crash. The chandelier fell and did indeed crush the crib. When she looked at the clock, it read 4:35. What most don't realize is that premonitions are actually very common and have been recorded throughout history. Many experiments have been conducted that continue to suggest that human beings really do have an innate ability to foresee the future.

Researchers have found that many trains or planes, which later crash, carried fewer passengers than usual. For example, the two aircrafts that flew into the World Trade Center on September 11th were said to be less crowded than normal. Was this due to a gut feeling or premonition? Or can it be chalked up to plain old luck? Many believe the odds are greater that the passengers had a subconscious hunch that something was about to happen.

Shelley E. Parker would certainly agree that intuition, not chance, was at play. As a children's author and psychotherapist, she has experienced many remarkable spiritual experiences ever since she was a child, including an NDE and many prophetic dreams. To begin our interview, she shared one of her premonitions.

> In mid-August 2009, when I was 37, after several months of having horrendous pain in my sternum and lower back, with awful but extremely brief episodes of flu-like symptoms and occasional blue lips, I was diagnosed with a very rare form of Burkitt's Lymphoma.
>
> When I was diagnosed, I was told I had around five weeks to live. The treatment was four months of aggressive chemotherapy, which would include eight rounds of intrathecal chemo. It was one of the most aggressive chemotherapy regimens used at the time.

My hematologist told me to go home, get my stuff, and go straight to the cancer ward. In addition, I was told to do this in under an hour, as they had to start the four months of very intensive chemotherapy immediately if I had any real chance of surviving.

Steven, my childhood sweetheart of 23 years, and I basically went into shock. We rushed home, got my stuff, went to the cancer ward, and then we sat on the bed, hugged each other, and cried.

The one thing that made it easier was the fact that, when I was 21, I dreamed I would get cancer in my mid-30s. I was told the type of cancer I would get, shown how I would feel, shown one of the procedures I would have, and also shown one of the doctors who would treat me—even down to being told what he would say to me, which, when I was seriously ill with pneumonia part way through my treatment, I mimed along with him as he said the words.

The main thing that sustained me all through the cancer treatment was that I was also shown in that dream I wouldn't die from the cancer. This dream was one of many prophetic dreams and experiences that I've had in my life.

In September 2009, Shelley had an unforgettable foretelling dream that changed her life. She was allowed to go home for a brief period prior to her next treatment. She was about five weeks into her chemotherapy regime and unbeknownst to her, very close to death. In fact, she was placed on the "very seriously ill" ward list and told that she might not survive the day. "I think this is the reason I had the dream I did the night before," she noted. "I was so close to death myself that perhaps I was more attuned."

The evening before she was to return to the hospital, Shelley's fiancé took her for a ride. Uncharacteristically, Steven spent a lot of time talking about God and what he felt awaited him. She said Steven considered himself spiritual and always believed in God, but was not a fan of organized religion. They also talked about their hopes for the future, but that future would never materialize.

That same night, I had one of the most "real" dreams I've ever experienced. Initially, I was in the upstairs room of a Methodist church, which I haven't been in since I was a child. God appeared but was unlike any image I've ever had of God. He was around 5-foot, 7-inches, very thin, and wearing a black suit with white pinstripes.

It was his face that was so surprising though: There was no face. Instead, there was a "cloud" of what looked like gray wool with silver tinsel, like streaks of silver electricity all through it and there were constant flashes of light and energy pulsing through the "wool."

God walked into the room (I knew with certainty that it was God but I don't know how) with another male figure, who was someone I still don't recognize from any scripture I've read. The man looked as though he was in his early 20s, mid-height. (This is strange but, even though I knew he was taller than God in my dream, he never seemed taller in the dream. This is rather hard to explain but, again, it's something I just "knew.")

The man seemed to be looking at me almost apologetically, but with so much compassion, as though he knew I was about to be told something horrendous.

The scene changed and I was suddenly in my local Anglican church and Steven and I were initially standing at the altar. It was as though Steven was in a trance. Although he was there, he didn't take part in the dream; he seemed almost frozen.

It switched again and I was in another part of the same church, which now has a profound resonance for me. God suddenly became huge and was so big that I could only see his face. His face changed into a normal man's face and now he was around his mid-30s with short, chestnut hair.

He looked at me and told me very matter-of-factly that Steven would die the next day. In that moment, I knew my fiancé and partner of 23 years was going to die and there was nothing I could do. I knew it was real and it was going to happen.

I started screaming and fell onto the church floor and started pleading with God, telling God I had cancer. He couldn't do that to me; I pleaded with God to let me die instead, because that's what people with cancer did and then Steven could keep living. I also remember swearing a lot at God and telling Him he had no right to take away the man I adored, especially when I loved him and needed him so much.

Through all of this, God was just looking at me, occasionally looking away, very calm and totally silent, waiting for me to calm down. Once I was a bit more lucid, God told me very patiently that it was the way it had to be and I'd always known Steven would die young, which I did, and that I had been warned when I first saw Steven, which was also true.

God said it was Steven's time to die and if everything went the way it was currently going and if Steven did the things he was currently doing, it would be the next day. This felt like free will to me in the dream. We have some things mapped out in our lives, but we always have free will.

Parker was warned that if she stopped Steven, a helicopter pilot, from flying the next day, he would then die two days later. She was also shown how he would die and told if she intervened, he would then die a painful death in a car crash. The accident, she was told, would happen on his way to the hospital to visit her. She was shown the accident scene in horrific detail.

In contrast, the younger man showed me how Steven's death would be if I said nothing to him. I was, at this point, also screaming at the younger man, who actually looked a bit scared (almost like an apprentice who has been told to take on a bit more than he's used to doing), but he also had a look of total and complete compassion on his face.

He began to tell me Steven would die in a helicopter crash but I already knew he would die like this, again from what I'd been told previously. I screamed at the man that I knew already how he would die.

He asked me if I wanted to feel what Steven would feel if I didn't tell him. Before I could answer, I experienced a sudden, very swift and strong downward rush of air, followed by a huge bump.

Just prior to this point, God had disappeared, walking out of the church and turning right, which had become the room above the Methodist church again.

Before He left, He gave me a look, which I have never forgotten. It was a look that I can only explain as that look that parents give a child when they've done something that they shouldn't: "I'm not angry; I'm just disappointed with you." I immediately knew why I was getting that look. It was partly because I knew Steven had only been on "loan" to me and so God was almost chastising me (in a compassionate way, though) for asking for more time.

The other reason was that I knew I wasn't doing as much in my life prior to the cancer that I should have been doing. It was a "Get your act together" kind of look as well.

At the end of the dream, I was in my mum's house, at the top of the stairs, again with the young man, who all this time had been holding something like a file. It's the look of compassion and also this lack of experience that I remember most from him, as though he was out of his comfort zone. At the same time, though, he was so professional and so kind.

The next morning, as Steven stood in front of her, Parker admits the urge was very strong to tell him about her dream but she didn't. She didn't, she said, simply because she was told not to. She also knew that prolonging his death would ultimately make things worse for him, so as hard as it was for her, she kept quiet.

Had she pleaded with him not to fly that day, Shelley believes he would have done so anyway. "Steven loved flying," she said. "He used to say he had two roles in life: to look after me and to fly helicopters. I've never regretted not telling him, not even for a second. Nothing I could have done would have prevented his death, no matter what I'd have done. I would have only ever postponed it."

In December 2009, three months after Steven's death, she was discharged from the hospital. She was extremely weak and still recovering from the effects of the harsh chemotherapy. One evening, as she sat watching television, her attention drifted to the bookshelves that stood to the left of her in the bedroom.

> As I was looking at the shelves, I felt myself start to feel as though I was floating up toward the ceiling. It felt very peaceful and I suddenly felt very happy and healthy. It was as though everything suddenly became perfect.
>
> At one point, I remembered that I was dying and it really didn't matter. The feeling was wonderful and I felt at peace and "one" with something, if that makes sense. As soon as I realized I was dying, however, the thought came to me that I couldn't do this to my mum because she had been through so much already. As soon as I had this thought, I was "dropped" back into my body and all those wonderful feelings were replaced with weakness and sickness once again.

At first, Parker was upset that the feelings of peace and happiness were gone, but at the same time, her NDE, like her prophetic dream, reaffirmed her belief in the afterlife. Interestingly, she feels that were it not for her dream about Steven she would have died.

> Had I not had that dream, I firmly believe I'd have just lost the will to live, and died. It would have been too difficult to cope

with the death of my soulmate while trying to deal with the cancer and the horrible chemotherapy regime.

It made me realize that there is a God, there is a Heaven, we don't really die, and our loved ones are still around us if we need to call on them. That's something I know with certainty.

In February 2015, Parker's hematologist gave her a clean bill of health. This is quite miraculous considering she was given just five weeks to live in August 2009. Speaking of her own intuitive sense, she said, "Coming so close to dying and losing my soulmate has made me even more intuitive and open to premonitions and the like. When you open your mind to this, life is actually easier, not harder. Anyone can do this. But you have to want to listen. You have to be open to the feelings and trust what you are given." Knowing of Steven's death in advance, she noted, made things a little easier to deal with. "I've felt a huge sense of calm since the dream. Death isn't scary anymore, and I know Steven is always with me."

Just as Parker finished writing "It made me realize that there is a God, there is a Heaven, we don't really die, and our loved ones are still around us if we need to call on them. That's something I know with certainty," she heard a helicopter fly over her house. She rushed to look outside; even though she could clearly hear the sound of a helicopter, there wasn't one in sight.

For more information about Shelley E. Parker, visit *www.shelleye parker.com.*

 ## It Wasn't a Dream

Jennie Taylor Martin, Virginia

My mother was diagnosed with lung cancer in 1992. Although it wasn't clear at the time, the cancer had already spread to other organs in her body. The next year she had surgery to remove one lung and basically never recovered.

Her condition continued to worsen and she ended up back in the hospital about 12 months later. My brothers and sisters and I were all there in her room, gathered around her bed, when she insisted that we all hold hands together and make a circle around her, which we did.

Suddenly, Mom began making strange movements with her arms—arms that she had previously been unable to lift due to the pain she felt as the cancer caused her body to atrophy. As we all watched, she raised her hands all the way to her forehead, and swung them quickly outward and away from the middle of her forehead. It was as if she was repeatedly clearing either her crown chakra or her third eye.

Watching her gave me the feeling that she was following instructions from some unseen teacher. At one point, my sister Bobbie leaned down to my mom's ear and began singing the song lyrics from On Holy Ground by Geron Davis: "And I know there are angels all around us. . . ."

As soon as the words were out of Bobbie's mouth, my mother started nodding and saying, "I know. Look!" She then pointed up to the ceiling in the corner of her hospital room. We all got chills as we looked up. Of course, we couldn't see what she was seeing. But there was no need to; we understood that she was seeing angels.

That night, I stayed with my sister in the very bed my mom had spent many months in following her surgery. Sometime after, I had a dream. I call it a "dream" for lack of a better word, but it wasn't really a dream. The best way to describe it is being awake while my eyes are closed.

It felt as though I was being squeezed by some unseen presence or force. This presence embraced my entire body—like a full body hug. I could feel what was happening, but I couldn't see a thing. There was no light, no figure of a person. Nothing.

Still in my dream, I asked, "Mom, is that you? Mom, I love you. I'll miss you. Goodbye!" Just as I said those words, I was awoken by the sound of the phone ringing. My sister answered.

It was the hospital calling to tell us that our mother had just passed. So again, I call my experience a dream because that's the closest word for it. But it wasn't a dream at all. It was my mother saying goodbye.

 ## She Would Get There When She Got There

P. Sawyers, Tennessee

My mother had cancer for a number of years. When the end was near, she was home under hospice care and we were taking turns (around our work schedules) caring for her. On this particular day, it was 3 or 4 a.m. and my mom was lying in bed mumbling to herself. She did this for a couple of hours straight. I asked her if she wanted anything, but she just replied that she was visiting with some people.

Having worked in a nursing home for many years, I knew people often talked to others while on their deathbed. So as I sat with my mother, I didn't think much of it.

Suddenly, while I was watching television in her room, she sat up and looked over at a chair in her room that she could never get rid of after my dad died. "Robert," she said, "I told you that I would be there in a little while." (Robert was my father's name.)

It was in the tone of voice I had heard her use so many times when I was a child and she was aggravated with my father about something. I looked over at the chair and knew she was seeing my father sitting there as he had done so many times before. My mom died a few hours later.

My father had died 19 years earlier, and I think he was there telling her to hurry because he missed her so much. But my mother made it clear that she would get there when she got there.

She Nodded Three Times

Melanie, New Jersey

My mother in-law, Lorraine, was in rehab and had pneumonia. Even though her son and I eventually divorced, we remained very good friends and I was still very close to his mother. I visited her almost every day. She was 88 years old at the time, but she was still very sharp for her age.

Lorraine remained active up until the end and was always there for everybody else. She had such a positive attitude and remained my best friend despite my divorce with her son. I continued to have a cordial relationship with the family and, as I said, she was very special to me.

She was in rehab and wasn't getting better, so they decided to transfer her back to the hospital. My ex-husband and I were there with her. Lorraine was in the ER and was trying to tell us something but couldn't. She was getting oxygen and the mask was covering her mouth.

I'm a nurse and needed to get to work at 11 p.m. that night, so we left, planning to come back the next morning. Soon after we left, however, the hospital called to tell us that her vital signs were not good and we were advised to come back.

When we returned to the hospital, Lorraine was intently looking straight ahead. We were called into the conference room and told that things were not good. My mother-in-law had COPD (chronic obstructive pulmonary disease), which is an inflammatory lung disease that causes congested airflow from the lungs. We were asked if we wanted Lorraine to be put on a breathing machine if needed, but we declined.

Her wishes were to not be kept alive by machines. The doctors warned us that her condition would surely worsen and that she probably had until sometime that morning.

We spent the entire night talking to her and trying to comfort her. They had her on comfort care, which is morphine and oxygen, but she was still observant. Her eyes were open and she was alert, staring intently straight ahead, but she did not seemingly respond to our questions. In fact, she didn't seem to be paying any attention to us. It was clear to me and my ex-husband that she saw something, but we had no idea what or who.

This went on for hours. Then around 8 a.m. that morning she again stared straight ahead, but this time she distinctly nodded her head three times. It was as though someone was asking her if she was ready to cross over. She visibly seemed to be answering someone. A short time later, she passed away.

After leaving the hospital, we drove to Lorraine's house, overcome with grief. We sat in the backyard thinking of her and recollecting fond memories. Suddenly, a red cardinal appeared. We looked at each other happily knowing this was a sign from Heaven. Lorraine may not have been able to talk to us on her deathbed, but she now found a way to let us know she was okay.

Author's Note: The red cardinal symbolizes life, death, and renewal, and is said to be a sign from the afterlife.

In the Light of Death

Ineke Koedam

After a career in business, Ineke Koedam's life took a major turn in 2000 when she decided to direct her attention to death and bereavement. As a former hospice coordinator, she now dedicates her time to helping others understand that dying is a transition rather than an end. Having worked with so many dying patients and witnessing many deathbed phenomena, she believes it is time that we become more sensitive to the dying process and that understanding the dying process will teach us invaluable lessons. It may even change our preconceived notions of life and death while expanding our awareness of a different reality.

In talking to Koedam, one can clearly see she is very passionate about her cause. It is also evident that her experiences have changed her in many ways. The author of *In the Light of Death*, Koedam admits this was never a book she had intended to write. But, as they say, things happen for a reason.

> In 2009, I met Peter Fenwick at a conference in the Netherlands. Fenwick was one of the preeminent speakers talking about his research on deathbed phenomena. I was one of the speakers, too. The more-than-interested audience encouraged Fenwick to pursue his research in the Netherlands. The next day I took Fenwick to the hospice where I had worked as a volunteer and hospice coordinator. It seemed obvious that I should carry on this research and that is what happened.
>
> The small-scale study I carried out in the Netherlands took place between 2009 and 2011. Thirty hospice caregivers from three different hospices took part. The study was comprised of two in-depth interviews per person. The first was after the participant filled in a questionnaire that looked back at experiences and observations of the preceding five years (retrospective study). The second, one year later, took place after filling in a questionnaire about experiences and observations for that particular year (prospective study).

At the conclusion of her work with Peter Fenwick, a renowned English neuropsychiatrist, she found herself with an abundance of amazing material and shared experiences.

> When I started to carry out Fenwick's research, I had no intention at all of writing a book about these experiences. It was only at the beginning of 2012 that the idea arose of letting hospice caregivers have their say, having heard only from the scientists so far, so I decided to put this precious material together in a book. No scientific statistics, but real experiences and observations of hospice staff who work on the boundary between life and death. We can learn so much from them

when it comes to observations and experiences of those who are dying.

This profound feeling may last from a few moments to hours. Most sensitive caregivers will not start with the after-care because they feel that they would be intruding in a process that was still going on. The process gradually lessens in intensity but may be felt for days. This presence after death is tangible by the atmosphere in the room, although not everyone seems to be receptive to this.

The presence of light appears to be a common link among many of these spiritual phenomena. Like so many who have had a near-death experience, a number of the dying witness the presence of light as well. Koedam adds, "So if the dying actually do experience light, we don't know. However, this light is often accompanied by feelings of intense peace, which is felt regularly. I am inclined to say that the above examples are shared experiences and that the dying indeed experience this light."

Deathbed phenomena, according to Koedam, provide invaluable messages of hope to both the living and the dying. For one, she notes, they continue to suggest that we never die alone. "The care for the dying (and for that matter the living) is far greater than we may think, and dying is not a lonely or fearful journey but an intensely hopeful one."

As noted earlier, Koedam began her research into deathbed phenomena in 2009 after meeting Dr. Peter Fenwick, a leading authority on near-death experiences and deathbed visitations. However, her interest in these spiritual experiences began long before her chance meeting with Fenwick. She admits that she has always had a deep interest in alternate realities. When she was 13, her paternal grandmother passed away. That evening, Koedam said, her grandmother's spirit came to visit her.

I don't believe I had more of a special bond with her than my two sisters had, but that evening she chose to visit me and sat at the foot of my bed. Back then this phenomenon was dismissed as some kind of make-believe and just an imagination, until I had another encounter with my grandmother, this time in a dream. I vividly remembered this so-called departing vision when I was in my teens.

This time I was 40 years of age. I had just started to work as a volunteer in a "home-from-home hospice" when I had this particular dream. I dreamed that my grandmother had been admitted to our hospice, which in the Netherlands we call an "almost-at-home home," and that I regularly checked on her whenever I was on duty. It was remarkable how beautiful and young she looked. One day she took me on an astral journey. In the distance I became aware of an incredibly beautiful city. A city of gold, a city of light, and I was heading toward this illuminating scene. Actually, I seemed to be drawn to it. But then, all of a sudden, there was this moment that I had to return and before I knew it, I was sitting again next to my grandmother in her hospice bed.

To me this was not only an imperative dream, but also a meaningful dream, indicating that my grandmother was almost home. And to my grandmother, almost home meant almost united with God. I was left with an indelible imprint.

Some speak of the idea of dying a good death, which basically means being prepared and dying the way one prefers to die. Preferences, of course, differ greatly, but an example would be having advanced directives in order and choosing to die at home. Koedam, however, disagrees with the idea of dying a good death. Paradoxically, she says letting go of the idea of dying a good death actually seems to ensure a good death.

Research has shown that people have different wishes and needs regarding death. Recognizing these differences as well as fulfilling the specific needs of the dying person in the final stages contribute to what many people would call a good death. However, accommodating these needs and wishes still doesn't say anything about a good death, while the nonfulfillment of these needs and wishes doesn't mean that it will not be a good death either. Time and again, I have seen that what is most essential about dying just cannot be directed by us. It is simply granted to us, if we find ourselves in the flow of serving the autonomic process that dying entails.

When we can let go of the idea of a good death because we realize that a good death comes from preconceived ideas, it gives us space. It is this space that allows us, when we die, to connect with our own inner truths, our true beings and surrender.

Throughout the years, her view of dying has changed in so many ways. Koedam has learned so much in working with the dying. For instance, she notes that we are far more than our physical bodies.

From the dying, I learned who we really are. I learned that the more we are able to connect with the spirit that we are, the more the identification with our physical bodies diminishes. Not only will our concern with illness and the fear of finiteness dissipate, we will also begin to look at life from a different perspective. Illness, aging, dying, and other events in life will become experiences of the soul rather than an irrevocable tragedy. Among other identifications, the physical is widespread. And mind you, identification limits us in realizing who we truly are. When we gain insight into who we really are, we won't be able to experience physical death other than a transition. Our body is mortal. Our true being is not.

I agree wholeheartedly with Koedam. In my book, *Make Up Your Mind to Be Happy*, I wrote about how we can all focus on the positives in any situation—even death. If more people could treat death with acceptance and not resistance, they would learn many illuminating lessons. Nothing teaches us more about life than death.

I guess I have always had a deep inner knowledge of alternate realities or different dimensions. At the same time I am a steadfast and down-to-earth woman, at least most of the time. I know that while we're here, we need to be here. In working in the hospice and caring for the dying, however, my sensitivity reemerged and I again became receptive to otherworldly realms.

My view of dying changed in a sense that now I feel that dying is a precious and essential process of every human being. A process which is also organic; that is, we can only surrender to it rather than control it. It is truly impressive to be a witness of the ego that is taken over by the soul, until life has been lived right up until the end and the dying are facing a new reality hidden in this passage. So last but not least I feel that dying is a transition. A transition to another dimension. As I said, our body is mortal, our true being is not.

For more information about Ineke Koedam, visit *www.ineke koedam.com.*

Who Is in the Back of the House?

Betty J. Kerling, Pennsylvania

I was working as a hospice aide and was told that one of my patients would most likely not make it through the night. As I pulled up to my patient's home, I had a good view of him through the window of the living room. As I got out of my car and walked up to the door, I could clearly see that he was having trouble breathing so I quickly rang the doorbell.

His wife answered the door and told me that her husband had been fine all day until I pulled up in the driveway. He passed six minutes later as his wife and I stood at his bedside. I called the agency to have them send over a nurse to pronounce him dead and record the time of death. As I waited, his wife told me that she didn't want to be alone when her husband passed. She was sure her husband knew this and had held on just long enough until I got there to make his transition. To me, this clearly showed that the dying sometimes have a say as to their time of death.

As a hospice worker, I've seen a lot of sick people pass on, but some affected me more than others. Once I was taking care of a woman who required a 24-hour watch. I was one of three aides taking care of her, each of us with eight-hour shifts. I had the 11 p.m. shift.

One night when I arrived, the aide that I was relieving told me that our patient's husband had died that day. He had a heart attack in their bedroom toward the back of the house. Soon after, all sorts of odd things began to happen. For instance, our patient began talking to people that no one else could see. When we questioned a family member about it, we were told that it was just her deceased husband making sure that his wife was taken care of.

I will never forget the day she passed away. I was sitting with her watching television. She kept moving her hand up as if someone was holding it and then putting it back down as if someone had let go. At this point, she was very ill. Her tongue was swollen and she was unable to talk.

On this particular day, I was working the first shift and she was holding hands with this imaginary person on and off. Suddenly, she looked at me and clearly asked, "Who is in the back of the house?" I thought I had misunderstood what she said so I asked her to repeat her question. She repeated again, "Who is in the back of the house?" In response, I told her that no one was in the back of the house and that it was only her and me. She did not believe me and replied, "Yeah, right!" I was startled by her words because, as I said before, she was not able to talk at this point.

It was obvious to me that she thought someone was in the bedroom. After my shift ended, I went home to get some sleep. I was just dozing off when the phone rang. It was the aide from the third shift telling me that the woman had passed away shortly after I left.

Was this woman's deceased husband there waiting for his wife? I have no doubt he was.

In the 1980s, my mother was in a coma for four days due to problems with her kidneys. She didn't tell me about her near-death experience until much later. She told me she had seen my deceased father in Heaven and he told her that she had to go back because it wasn't her time.

What these experiences clearly tell me is that you go to a better place after you die and you are with your loved ones. This I know with my heart and soul.

 ## Aunt Terry

Nancy Redmond, Minnesota

My mother's sister (I called her my Cutie Pie Aunt Terry) was diagnosed with stage four ovarian cancer in 2007. It was a long, hard journey for her. After her first surgery, she never recovered strength or any reasonable quality of life. As Aunt Terry neared the end of her battle, she was under hospice care and was living with her daughter, my cousin, Karen, who took such amazing care of her.

As the end drew near, Aunt Terry's granddaughter was scheduled to graduate from high school, and the family planned a celebration for her. Since Aunt Terry could not be left alone, my mom and I were asked to stay with her while the rest of the family attended the graduation ceremony. Those hours were a treasure for my mom and me.

It was clear to my mom and me that my aunt, though still here physically, was actually in the spiritual realm. Toward the end of our watch, she clearly looked into the corner of the room and said, "Oh, Hi, Jesus!" and smiled with the biggest smile I've ever seen on her beautiful face. It was truly amazing. It felt as if the veil between this life and that on the Other Side was thrown aside and Aunt Terry was able to see the glorious place that was the next stop on her journey.

Aunt Terry passed away the next day. My mom and I both knew who was waiting to escort her to the Other Side when she stepped out of her human existence.

I was fortunate enough to witness the same phenomenon again when my grandmother was on her deathbed. My husband, Kevin, and I spent many hours with her at the hospital knowing these were our last days with her. One day, toward the end of her life, as Kevin and I were sitting with her, she looked suddenly at both of us with the clearest blue eyes and huge smile and said, "Do you hear that music?"

Neither of us heard the music, but we never doubted for a second that she was hearing music from the angelic realm. The music was to welcome my grandmother back home. She passed two days later.

The memories of time spent with these two beautiful ladies—now angels—are the memories that hold me up in my darkest hours.

I Don't Want to Go

Lakisa Robinson, New York

I lost my mother on December 6, 2014, from cancer complications at just 56 years old. She had been fighting cancer for three years. I wanted to share an experience I had the night before my mother passed. That night, I stayed at the hospital with her.

It was one of those moments I will never forget. We talked; we held hands. Then she asked if she could sleep next to me. I held her all night long in my arms.

At one point she said, "I have to get my health together or I'm going to die." In response, I told my mother that she was going to be okay. "We just have to fight this pneumonia and start treatments." It was clear to me that she wanted to get better.

But later, out of nowhere, she told me, "This will be the last time I go through this with you." I was taken aback by her words and knew this was not coming from my mother. I truly believe Jesus spoke through my mother to let me know this night would be our last time together. I kept praying to Him before this happened. I pleaded, "Please don't take her" and He answered.

The next day, my mother had her eyes closed and was resting. Abruptly, she very clearly said three times softly, "I don't want to go." It was as if someone was talking to her. She then opened her eyes and screamed loudly, repeating, "I don't want to go." I quickly ran to her and said, "Mom, NO!" At that point, I knew what was going to happen from what I was told the night before.

She placed her hand over her chest and said, "My heart." Her eyes rolled back in her head as she started gasping for air. I immediately began praying. The hospital staff allowed me to stay in the room while they tried to revive her. After about eight minutes, she was stable enough to move to the intensive care unit. All the while, they continued to work on her.

A short time later, I heard over the speaker, "Code Blue, ICU!" This was my mother. She had just passed away. I went to see her in the intensive care unit after she passed. She looked so peaceful; a smile was now spread across her face. I knew then that she was in a better place.

I will never forget my mom's final moments and will always miss her dearly. But I will say that I find comfort in knowing that she is now at peace.

Dying to See Angels

Dr. John Lerma

John Lerma, MD, is no stranger to deathbed visits. As a hospice and palliative care physician, he is well known for his compassion for the terminally ill, as well as his work teaching others about end-of-life care. He is board certified in both internal medicine and hospice and palliative medicine.

A best-selling author, Dr. Lerma serves as a consultant to several hospices and palliative units in Houston and San Antonio, Texas. In his book, *Learning From the Light*, he shares the incredible story of a blind cancer patient named Sarah who was diagnosed with an aggressive form of breast cancer at the age of 29.

The story opens with Sarah as a little girl visiting St. Peter's Basilica in Rome with her mother. While there she has an encounter with an angel named Cherin and also meets the late Pope John Paul II. The following is her experience in Rome told to Dr. Lerma.

> The Pope greeted all of us, and, with immense compassion and empathy, he gently held me and placed my head on his chest over his heart, and just loved me. As tears began to flow down my face, I remember he gently placed a finger on my cheek and let one tear roll onto his finger. He then whispered into my ear, "My child, this teardrop holds the faith needed to heal you in ways you cannot imagine. God has sent an angel to guard you and guide you as you prepare to glorify him through a miraculous life. You will help many come to believe in an all-loving God, Sarah. Like you, I could be healed from my ailments, but we are being asked to view suffering for its strength and not its weakness. You see, Sarah, Jesus' plan is to bring all souls back home, but he needs the empowering innocence of children and their willful suffering to engender his design. Pray for understanding and wisdom, my child.

Sarah went on to live a challenging life, as both her parents passed from cancer before she even celebrated her 26th birthday, leaving her no choice but to live alone. As she lay in a hospice hospital bed tired and spent, she was again visited by the angel of her youth named Cherin.

Dr. Lerma, I know my time is nearing, so please stop all remaining chemotherapy and radiation treatments. I want to be as alert as possible the last few weeks of my life, as I want to see God's angels with my eyes. Cherin came back last night and told me he and so many other angels, as well as my parents, would be coming soon to present a gift from God.

Dr. Lerma visited with Sarah often and had several profound conversations with her. The following dialogue is an excerpt from *Learning From the Light*.

So, tell me about the angels, Sarah.
Well, there was something different in the vibrations of the room last night. It was very similar to the sounds and vibrations I heard and felt when I was at St. Peter's Basilica in Rome. After a few minutes, I heard Cherin and four other angels. They were very comforting, so I was able to feel their feathers brushing up against my body and face. I remember they smelled like roses, which I love. Music also seemed to follow them, much like what I experienced in Rome. These sounds were much more engaging and full of the same ingredients of the music I heard at the Basilica: love, peace, hope, joy, and forgiveness. I guess these gifts and attributes have their own frequencies. A beautifully soft, loving voice then came through the music. It was from a woman. She took my hand, placed it on her heart, and said, "Sarah, you will see with your eyes before you return home. However, we need to prepare your mind and cells to be able to respond to what it

sees without displeasure and confusion. With your hand over my heart, I am facilitating these actions. What would normally take weeks to months will only take seconds to hours."

Sarah: Who are you? Were you the mother on the statue I stood in front of while in Rome? You must be Mary, Mother of God.

Angelic woman: I am the woman on the statue when you visited Rome.

Sarah: You mean you are Mary. The mother of Jesus Christ?

Angelic woman: Yes, I am, dear. You invited the angels and me into your heart and soul long ago, and we have been waiting to make ourselves known to you. You have done well, my dear. Many have been saved because of your selfless actions, and now God has many gifts for you; the first being sight of the world you will be leaving. The next has been made known to you years ago. We are here to guide you back home where you will be with your mother, father, and friends. So much more is waiting for you, my dear."

Sarah: What is waiting for me, Mary?

Mary: Only God can tell you, but know this, my dear: It is beyond anything your heart could ever imagine, or all the souls could ever create. It will not entail pain or suffering. Sarah, remember this and pass it on to those who are caring for you. Understand that one does not need to see with one's eyes to be able to live on Earth, to have a family, a job, enjoy life, and have a dream. Having sight is the one human sense that is so rewarding if used correctly, but treacherous, as it can steer one in the wrong direction.

Sarah: Mary, before you leave, could you tell me what I will see when I am given the gift of sight?

Mary: Like I said earlier, you will see your parents, the multitude of angels, Jesus, many other spirits, and myself.

You will initially see your soul as God formed it. You will see your acknowledgment in its role for your Father's loving plan in reuniting all souls. You will also see the birth of the universe, the birth of your world, the birth of life, and finally your birth. The images will be soft and obscure at first, but will progressively brighten as your mind connects the new pictures and the previous images created by your functioning sense of sound, taste, smell, and touch.

We must leave now, Sarah. We love you with the love of God himself. You will begin to see slowly through the next few weeks. Pray for all the souls around you and throughout God's Creation, so that they will be in line with the will of the Father of Love, Forgiveness and Peace.

I felt them hug and kiss me, like you kissed me the other night. Yes, Dr. Lerma I was not totally asleep.

Sarah, could you tell me if there are angels around us now and, if so, what they look like?

I feel totally energized and joyful, because there are so many angels around me. Each one is different. That's sort of cool. I would say their heights range from 4 feet to more than 10 feet, as the taller ones appear to be extending past the ceiling, which I think is 10 feet. Some have long blond hair, others short dark hair, and most of their eyes are blue, with a few of the taller ones having light brown to hazel-looking eyes. Their attire, if you will, consists of long, flowing robes, which seems to be silk-like in texture and snow white in color. None of the ones that are present have feathered wings; however, I am told that they do exist. The angels around us at this time appear to be floating in mid-air, and, as they center and leave our dimension, they evoke an immensely bright light, which leaves a form of static electricity throughout the room. I wish you could see them, Dr. Lerma.

Have you seen your parents? Do they look younger?
I saw them a few days ago and was told they would return tonight to guide me back home. They looked to be in their late 20s to early 30s, healthy, and extremely happy and content.

Do you know anything about the gift God is going to give you?
I thought it was my sight, but the angels told me it's something else. You know something, Dr. Lerma? Some of the angels are really jokesters, and laugh a lot. They like it when we laugh. They say it is really healing and a sign of innocence, joy, compassion, and healing. Comedians are said to be inspired by angels, but many veer toward using the gift with negativity. Jesus loves to laugh, and wants us to learn to laugh effortlessly and frequently.

I noticed that Sarah was growing tired, but still comfortable, so I told her I wanted her to get some rest and we would continue our discussion tomorrow. I left Sarah late that evening filled with love, joy, laughter, and forgiveness, and for that I would always be grateful.

It was now Easter Sunday, around 4 a.m., when my phone awakened me. I was in a deep sleep and having a flying dream where my three children, Mark, Daniella, and Arianna, and I were laughing uncontrollably as we proceeded to cover the White House with purple toilet paper. I continued laughing even after I woke up. I've always loved those kinds of dreams. The funny thing is that my kids and I would probably do something like that, given the opportunity.

Sarah's nurse was calling to tell me that she had passed away peacefully with a smile on her face at 3:55 a.m. The nurse told me the following: "After you left last night, Dr. Lerma, Sarah and I spoke a bit as I washed her hair. In that conversation she said she wanted me to write a message for you so you would never forget her and the gift. "Dr. Lerma, I am very tired now, and because you knew I would be gone before your hospital rounds, I wanted to tell you that Jesus was here the whole time you and I were talking about the angels. He was sitting next to you and his energy was what gave us both total peace and comfort. The gift was on the other side of the bed, and his name was John. Yes, John Paul II. He showed me my tears that were still on his fingers and palms from my visit to Rome. When he rubbed them on my eyes, I was able to see infinitely more. I was looking at the kingdom of God. It was so worth it.

Did Sarah dream those experiences or did she actually see these angelic figures with her own eyes? In answer to this question, let me first say that it is not possible that Sarah could have dreamed of these images because the blind do not experience imagery in their dreams. What we experience in our dreams is our subconscious mind sorting through visual memories. The blind have no visual memories, with the exception of those who became visually impaired after birth.

Psychologists Kenneth Ring and Sharon Cooper conducted an in-depth study of the near-death experiences of the blind. The study determined that the blind do in fact see for the first time during their NDEs, but lose their sight once they return to their body.

One of Ring and Cooper's most compelling cases was a woman named Vicky who was born blind. Following an automobile accident, Vicki found herself floating above her body in the hospital emergency room and was able to describe her surroundings in detail. "I had a hard time relating to it (seeing) . . . because I've never experienced it. It was something very foreign to me. It was like hearing words and not being able to understand them, but knowing that they were words. But it was something new, something you'd not been able to previously attach any meaning to."[1]

Perhaps the late Dr. Elizabeth Kubler-Ross, a Swiss-born American psychologist, explained it perfectly: "People after death become complete again. The blind can see, the deaf can hear, cripples are no longer crippled after all their vital signs have ceased to exist."

Excerpt from *Learning From the Light* is reprinted with permission of New Page Books, Wayne, NJ. All rights reserved. 2007.

Take My Hand

Barbara, Tennessee

My husband died of cancer in 2005. At the time, we had a bed set up in the living room for him. The night that he passed away, he kept looking at the corner of the room. This went on for quite some time. Suddenly, he tried to get out of bed. I went over to help him lay back down because he was just too weak to get up. I knew if he did get up, he would fall.

My husband told me that he wanted to go with him. I asked who he was talking about but he only looked passed me. As I was trying to get him to lay back down, he sat back up again looking in the corner and held out his hand saying, "Take my hand."

Thinking he was talking to me, I took his hand but he jerked his hand from mine and said, "Not you." Then he once again looked in the corner of the room, held out his hand, and said, "Please, take my hand."

He sat back up while still holding out his hand. He then suddenly had the most peaceful look on his face, laid back down on the bed, and was gone. I will never forget this experience for as long as I live. I would give anything to have my husband back again, but I know he is no longer in any pain. For this I am happy because he had been in so much agony for so long.

That day my sister kept me company and spent the night with me. We pulled out the sofa bed in the living room because I didn't want to sleep in the bedroom. We then turned the light off and were almost asleep when the light unexpectedly turned back on again all by itself. There was no one else in the room but us.

It freaked my sister out but it didn't scare me. I just smiled to myself knowing it was my husband letting me know he was okay.

 ## Send Me Pink Roses

Susan, California

My sister was dying of breast cancer. We lived thousands of miles apart; she was in Washington and I was in California. I would talk to my sister as often as I could by phone, especially when she was coming to the end of her cancer battle. She was in so much pain.

During one of our last conversations, I asked her if she was seeing people and relatives who had passed on and also asked if they wanted her to come with them. In response, my sister said that she was seeing deceased loved ones. I told her that she should go with them—one of the hardest things that I ever had to say. I just didn't want my sister to suffer anymore.

I then asked her to do me a favor. "Linda, send me pink roses so I know you are doing well." She told me she would, and I even asked her to promise to do so, which she did. I told no one about my secret request except for my husband. I didn't want him to send me pink roses during that time. Exactly one month after my sister's death I received a big bouquet of flowers at the bank where I work from a customer. I had helped him with his bank account and the flowers were his way of showing his appreciation.

At the time, I didn't think much of it. There were all sorts of flowers in the arrangement. But when I called to thank him, I wasn't prepared for what he said: "You know when I walked into the florist something told me to get you pink roses. I walked up and down the rows of arrangements but I didn't see any pink roses. So I asked the florist to please add some pink roses to the arrangement I had picked out. So please notice the pink roses in there."

When he said this, I couldn't even breathe. I just cried because I knew then that it was my sister letting me know that she was fine and doing well. I still get tears in my eyes every time I think of those beautiful flowers.

 ## Nonna

The dying appear to have a say in when they depart their bodies. There have been several reports in which the dying have said things like "Hold on. I just want to say goodbye first," only to pass shortly afterward. Also, many choose to cross over when their loved ones leave the room. I've seen it many times in my own family. When my grandmother was in the hospital after having a heart attack, she told my mother to go home and get some rest. Shortly after, she took a turn for the worse and passed.

I can still remember almost every detail of my maternal grandmother's death. A college student at the time, I was haunted by the thoughts of an upcoming statistics test. I had been studying for hours but nothing seemed to stick.

Suddenly the phone rang, breaking my trance and giving me a break from my studies. It was my cousin, Louie.

"Josephine," he screamed. "Nonna, Nonna!"

"Louie, what's wrong?"

"She's dying. She's upstairs and she said she's dying."

The phone hit the floor. I ran upstairs as fast as I could. "Mom," I yelled, "something is wrong with Nonna."

By the time I reached the top of the steps, my mother was out of bed and dressed. My sister rushed outside to get her car. My grandmother lived only three and a half blocks away. We got there in less than one minute, but it seemed like forever.

My grandmother was clutching the bedpost as she struggled to talk to my mother. "Anna," she said, "I'm going to die."

When the paramedics arrived, my grandmother refused to go the hospital; she said she would never come home. Despite our pleas, the paramedics said they could not take her against her will.

By 3 a.m., I felt nauseous and overcome with anxiety. I had watched my grandmother's body in continuous agitation for four hours. My mother finally convinced me to go home. At 8 a.m., my mother called. My grandmother had a heart attack, but I was told not to worry as she was in stable condition at nearby St. Elizabeth's Hospital.

I decided to go to the hospital after taking my test. But when I got to school, I couldn't concentrate on anything except my grandmother. At the time, I had no idea what to think. I felt an unmistakable heaviness that I could not explain. Breathing became a chore as I struggled to concentrate on my test.

Feeling that I had to get to the hospital as soon as possible, I walked up to Professor Geiger with my uncompleted test and explained. She understood and told me I could make it up on a later date. I ran to my car—my eyes wet with tears. As I drove to the hospital, my tears turned to sobs. Somehow I knew my grandmother had just passed. Somehow I knew her spirit was there saying goodbye to me one last time.

The hospital parking lot was full, but at this point I didn't want to waste another minute. I pulled into a fire zone and rushed through the main entrance. The woman at the front desk told me to go to the family waiting room on the fourth floor. When the elevator door opened, I spotted my Aunt Paulina crying at the end of the hallway.

"What is it?" I screamed. I ran into my grandmother's room. A nurse was yelling behind me, but I didn't stop. My grandmother was there, but she didn't look at me with her beautiful blue eyes. I never saw them again. I pushed my way past yet another nurse. "Leave me alone," I yelled. "She's my grandmother." I picked up her hand; it was cold.

"Is she dead?" I asked. "Is she?" The nurse did not answer. She didn't have to. I already knew the answer. As I was sitting in class struggling to complete my math exam that day, my grandmother was transitioning from this world into the next. Although I could not grasp what happened to me at the time, I now know I experienced what is known as a shared-death experience (SDE).

A few days after my grandmother's funeral, my mother told me about an experience she had at my grandmother's deathbed that night. According to her, my grandmother repeatedly gazed at one corner of the room like she was looking at someone. My mother noticed but didn't say anything at first. Then my grandmother said something that caught my mother off-guard: "Anna, your father is here."

My mother was confused; her father had passed away nearly 30 years ago. She asked my grandmother what she was talking about. My grandmother then went on to tell my mother that my grandfather was actually standing in the room with them. "He's right over there, Anna." My mother and everyone else in the room could not see him. Yet my grandmother insisted that he was there. What makes this deathbed experience even more intriguing is the fact that two weeks before her death, my grandmother told my cousin that my grandfather had come to her. Deathbed visits can occur minutes, hours, and even weeks before an impending death.

A Shared-Death Experience

Have you ever had a feeling that something was wrong or felt ill for no reason and couldn't figure out why, only to learn later that a loved one passed on? These experiences are known as a shared-death experience or empathic experience. When these experiences occur, one or several people share in the death or transition of the dying individual. Those who experience it can be in the same room as the dying person or, as you'll see in Annie Cap's case, thousands of miles away. Although the term was coined by best-selling author and renowned researcher Dr. Raymond Moody, the phenomenon has been recorded since the late 1800s.

A philosopher, physician, and psychologist, Dr. Moody has spent more than 40 years studying the afterlife and what happens when we die. In 1975, he published the first of several groundbreaking books, *Life After Life*, in which he introduced the term *near-death experience*, or *NDE*, and shared various accounts from around the world.

In addition to NDEs, Dr. Moody went on to research deathbed visits—particularly the shared-death experience (SDE). His work led to the release of his book, *Glimpses of Eternity*, which was co-written with Paul Perry. In it, he shares the story of a woman named Dana, who not only shared her husband's deathbed experience, but also witnessed his life review.

After feeling her husband Johnny's spirit go through her body, Dana noted that the hospital room was instantly swallowed up in a bright, white light and became replaced with what she described as a "wraparound" life review.

> Everything we ever did was there in the light. Plus I saw things about Johnny . . . I saw him doing things before we were married. You might think that some of it might be embarrassing or personal, and it was. But there was no need for privacy, as strange as that might seem. These were things that Johnny did before we were married. Still, I saw him with girls when he was very young. Later, I searched for them in his high school yearbook and was able to find them, just based on what I saw during the life review during his death.[1]

Dana goes on to explain that a child she and her husband lost during a miscarriage appeared and embraced them both.

> She was not a figure of a person exactly as you would see a human being, but more the outline of a sweet, loving presence

of a little girl. The upshot of her being there was that any issues we ever had regarding her loss were made whole and resolved.[2]

In 2010, my book *Visits to Heaven* was released by Fourth Dimension Press. My book highlights various near-death experiences from across the globe, much like Moody's *Life After Life*. The life review is one of several common characteristics associated with the NDE. Others include:

- The feeling of peace.
- Seeing a tunnel.
- Experiencing several after-effects (losing the fear of death).
- Having an out-of-body experience (OBE).
- Having a sense of being dead.
- Encountering a Supreme Being or Being of Light.
- Seeing relatives, friends, angels, and others.
- Not wanting to come back.

These traits are also experienced by those on their deathbed. The NDE seems to teach others how to fulfill their life's purpose and live happier lives. The SDE, however, prepares and comforts the dying and their loved ones prior to death.

Annie Cap

In her wonderful book, *Beyond Goodbye*, Annie Cap describes her personal struggle to understand a shared-death experience with her mother, who lay dying in a hospital bed more than 5,000 miles away. Although her experience and its after-effects truly changed her, Cap later realized that her mother's spirit was able to reach out and connect with hers even though they were far apart from each other in body. (Her mother, Betty, was in the United States while Cap was in the United Kingdom.)

It all began about 20 minutes before her death and, while I'm positive that the death of anyone's loving mother is bound to have a massive impact on them, the death of mine was like some kind of initiation. I suspect, without knowing it, my mom left me a priceless parting gift, a kind of booby prize of limitless value, although there's never been a day that I haven't wished for her physical presence instead.

It may sound trite but my life truly has never been the same since that cold day. It was the 2nd of January 2004, four in the afternoon at my house in England (GMT, Greenwich Mean Time)—almost 8 a.m. (Pacific, West Coast Time) in Portland, Oregon, where my mother was.

I was busy working upstairs with a client in my in-house therapy room, when suddenly out of the blue I began uncontrollably gagging and coughing. I could hardly breathe and I felt like I was drowning or suffocating. It came on without warning, from out of nowhere, so extreme and intense. I was wheezing and had a strange gurgling cough. Nothing I did seemed to stop it fully. Tears ran down my face as I tried to catch my breath in front of my client. I excused myself and rushed to the downstairs bathroom. I was trying to get as far away from my therapy room as I could. I didn't want him to hear me as I attempted to cough up whatever it was that was causing this.

I'm not sure what I had thought I could do about it, but I remember feeling a bit like a cat trying to vomit up a hair ball. I had no luck. My deliberate attempts to cough something up didn't help much. It was strange, especially since I didn't have a winter cold or anything wrong with me when it started. In fact, as far as I knew, I was in perfect health.

I began to feel quite scared when I realized that I couldn't ease the gagging sensation. The coughing wasn't so bad but the feeling of suffocation was horrible. My face was visibly wet with tears when I returned to my therapy room, and I felt myself getting more and more upset in front of my client. I was now feeling very emotional and overwhelmed. I continued to struggle to catch my breath, although I knew I wasn't actually choking. (I'd choked once in a ski resort cafeteria. Luckily I received the Heimlich maneuver. After the ordeal, my life-saver informed me of one very important distinction: You can't speak if you are truly choking.)

As I couldn't effectively clear whatever was going on with my throat and lungs, but I could talk, I knew I had no option but to stop the session. This had been my third appointment that day. However, when this client arrived, I recognized my heart wasn't in it. As soon as I made that decision to postpone the session, I sensed it was the right thing to do. Immediately, my mind then shifted to thoughts of my mother. I wanted nothing else but to be with her.

Sunrise was getting closer and closer to my mother as she lay in her hospital room in the states. We'd agreed to talk again as soon as morning had reached her bedside. I'd promised her the night before that I'd ring as soon as she was awake.

After ending her therapy session and showing her client to the door as fast as she could, Cap ran to the phone to dial her mother's hospital room. When she did, her sister Claire answered the phone and her coughing and gagging amazingly stopped.

While Claire quietly greeted me, I couldn't help but hear the gurgling and choking in the background. It was unbelievable and sounded exactly like what I had sounded like only minutes earlier. A chill ran through me. I had pins and needles up and down my spine as I made the association of what had just happened from so far away.

I feel now that she had attempted to link her remaining, drowning energy with mine to say goodbye and to hold me one last time. She must have truly wanted me to be with her as she was dying. That thought makes me even more sad and regretful that I hadn't flown out immediately. I should have gone. However, I'm sure that because of this experience, she knew how much I wanted to be with her, too. In this very unique and special way, she helped me be there.

I still don't understand how she did what she did—linking in with me—but she did it. So much more is possible than we know or can prove scientifically. Our experiential knowledge must be taken into consideration. It was obvious to me what had happened once I heard my mom's breathing and gagging when I called. This was confirmed again when I listened to what Claire had to say about my mom's long last night, as she struggled and postponed her death. I must have died a little along with her, feeling what she felt physically as she bridged time and space to get to me. And again, if she hadn't reached out to me, extending her consciousness in such an extreme way, I wouldn't have been able to say goodbye.

In addition to being an author, Cap is a holistic coach and therapist. For more information, visit *www.anniecap.co.uk/*.

William Peters

In 1998, William Peters was deeply affected by the death of his paternal grandmother, who deteriorated slowly after spending five years in a nursing home. Peters noted that she was somewhat demented and slept most of the day toward the end. During a visit with her during the last week of her life, however, she was surprisingly alert and coherent.

As I walked into Nano's room, I felt like I was barging into a conversation between my grandmother and some other people. She did not notice that I had entered her room as she spoke in an animated way that I had not seen in her for years. She was deeply engaged in a dialog and she appeared to be staring right at them. I looked around but could not see anyone else present in the room. I did not interrupt as I noticed how intent she was. As I listened, I realized she was speaking with her deceased relatives and friends.

She was so happy and it seemed to me that she was working some things out with these visitors that involved preparing her for what lay ahead. At the time, I didn't know if she was reviewing memories of her current life with these people or if she was imagining these lovely visitors who seemed to be her guides for the journey after this life. I learned later, and would observe frequently in my later work in hospice, that these experiences are commonly referred to as pre-death visions and routinely discounted by Western medical institutions as hallucinations.

Two years after his grandmother's death, Peters joined the Zen Hospice Project in San Francisco as a volunteer hospice worker. It was there that an encounter with a dying patient changed the course of his life. Paul (his name has been changed to protect his privacy), a former merchant marine, was suffering from stomach cancer and had few visitors. As a result, Peters made every effort to spend as much as three hours per visit at Paul's bedside talking and often reading to him. On this particular day, he read passages from *The Call of the Wild* by Jack London—one of Paul's favorites.

Paul was semi-conscious and struggled to hang on as the words of Jack London filled the room, but his fight would soon end. What happened next is, according to Peters, difficult to describe with words.

Suddenly, I realized I was floating, indeed suspended above my body. Paul was right next to me and we were looking at each other. Paul acknowledged that I was there with this kind of smug look on his face as if to say, "Check this out." A few moments later I was back in my body and reading to Paul. Honestly, I don't think I ever stopped reading to him.

His eyes were closed and he made no gesture to acknowledge this experience, and at the time I did not know how to make sense of it. Looking back, I think it was an act of love. I believe Paul invited me in because he was showing me where he was going. He was saying, "Hey, I'm still alive!" I don't know how this happened, but I do know from my research that the person who is transitioning seems to have the capacity to initiate a sharing of the deathbed experience.

When Peters came back to his body, he looked over at Paul's body and noticed something that wasn't there before. Although Paul made no acknowledging gesture, there was a tear running down his face.

At the time, I was still reading *The Call of the Wild*. Coincidently, at that same moment, I was reading about how the lead dog in the story becomes injured and old and has to be put to sleep. It's all very synchronistic. Like the dog in the story, Paul had lived a meaningful life but now was being put to sleep. On an unconscious level, I think that tear falling down Paul's face was his way of acknowledging that he was dying.

I later tried to share this experience with my Buddhist supervisor and he smiled and said, "It's all just phenomena rolling by, let it go." And so I did, at the conscious level, but I would have similar experiences with the dying and their loved ones on the hospice ward. I, like many hospice workers, cherished the time when the dying process approached that moment of transition because of the mystical nature of this experience.

The experience was over in an instant and Paul passed soon after. However, Peters was forever changed and would later find out that what he had experienced that day did indeed have a name: a shared-death experience.

I couldn't help but wonder what other experiences Peters had witnessed. He thought back to another memorable patient. Jack, he explained, had been in a semi-coma for about 90 days and never got out of bed. All the hospice workers who cared for him assumed his death was imminent. "But one day he just hopped out of bed," Peters recalled. "There were two or three of us there and we were just shocked. We were like, *Jack is out of bed. What is going on here?*"

Peters said the patient seemed very agitated as they tried to calm him down. "I asked him what he was doing, to which he replied, 'They're coming for me. I have to get going. I have to get my suitcase. They're waiting for me.'"

It was clear to everyone present that Jack was searching for his suitcase, as he felt he was going on a journey. (The feeling of an impending journey is actually a very common attribute of deathbed phenomena.) Jack passed within a week after the incident. "Deathbed visions seem to be closely correlated with the time at which you die," said Peters. "I think they are more noticeable as you get closer and closer to death. These visits can appear in a more subtle form in advance. They are not as dramatic."

As one gets closer and closer to death, Peters believes that the veil between the here and the hereafter gets thinner and opens up more and more. As a result, the dying person's energy is more focused on the transition and there are more external signs. "One of the most common signs you'll see is a person reaching up. I've seen it about a hundred times. They begin to reach for something and their eyes often appear fixated on something in the upper part, near the ceiling, of the room."

Unfortunately, noted Peters, many do not know how to react or engage in these situations. What hospice workers and others present should do is try to participate in the moment by asking common questions such as:

1. I noticed that you are looking intently at someone or something. Can you tell me who or what you see?
2. I noticed that you are reaching out your arms. Can you share with me what is happening?
3. I happened to hear you speaking to someone. Can you tell me who you are speaking with and what is being said?

Peters noted it is best to support these deathbed visits by protecting them from interruptions or distractions.

In addition to witnessing many deathbed and other spiritual phenomena, Peters also had two near-death experiences. I asked how these experiences have changed his view of life.

> We are confined and limited by our human body and our brain while on this earth. The idea of our existence is far greater than we could ever comprehend.
>
> I find that this world we live in is actually very relational. In other words, it is loving; it has a kind design. Yes, there is a lot of pain and suffering but it's still based on a kind, loving design. Living on Earth provides opportunities for learning and evolving but the lessons are hard for many of us. My body has been broken and has felt a lot of pain but when I just allow it and give it space, it's taught me my greatest lessons.

Peters is a licensed marriage and family therapist. In 2011, he founded the Shared Crossing Project to raise awareness and help educate the public about various afterlife phenomena. By teaching people about these end-of-life experiences, the Shared Crossing Project helps both the dying and their loved ones understand that consciousness does in fact live on. For more information, visit *www.sharedcrossing.com*.

My Sister Came for Dad

Pamela, Canada

My father had always been a very hard-working man, operating his own successful business in a technical field. He was extremely conservative, intelligent, well-read, well-traveled, worldly, and proud. He was also very dignified in his manners and always well-dressed when out and about in the city.

Having said that, he was very serious and would only believe that which could be proven. He was not at all inclined to fantasies or even considering the possibility of truth in strange or unconventional phenomena such as the paranormal. So when he came to me and told me about his "strange" ethereal experiences, I knew he was not one to make these things up. In fact, I highly doubt he believed in these experiences before he had his own.

In the late 1980s he suffered an aortic aneurysm rupture. I have learned that it is extremely rare for anyone to survive such a life-threatening condition. Months later, he told me that he had a near-death experience during the surgery.

His spirit, he said, lifted off the operating table looking down at his lifeless body. The chief surgeon sliced him open and my dad heard him exclaim, "What a mess!" My father then waved "bye-bye!" to his body, as he floated further up and then was being pulled down a tunnel toward a white light.

I had read accounts like this before, and had my doubts that this was really true. But after his experience, the remarkable change in my father told me that it was very real and true. Although he would not talk about how his NDE changed him, he became a more relaxed man, not as serious or intense. He also quit drinking completely. There was definitely something more spiritual, softer about his demeanor.

So 11 years later, when he experienced a deathbed visit, I once again had no doubt that what he had experienced was very real. As you can imagine, he needed a lot of blood during the aortic aneurysm surgery. It was later found that some of the blood given to him was tainted and he contracted hepatitis B, which ultimately led to liver cancer. I will not go on at length about his illness, but it was extremely painful for us to see him deteriorating so much at the end. When I thought he could not look any worse, the disease made him look even more hideous the following day. This monster was eating him alive from the inside out and it was very difficult. I was mad at God for keeping him alive and letting him suffer even after he expressed a wish to be put out of his misery.

We hardly had time to mourn my sister's sudden, violent death just over six months earlier, and I knew that part of my father's illness was also caused by his broken heart. The pain we were all going through was almost unbearable, which made the spiritual presence, when it came, that much more palpable and meaningful.

My father was taken care of by a wonderful group at the Salvation Army Grace Hospital in Ottawa, Ontario, Canada. They had immense compassion for not only my father but all of us. We were allowed to stay with him as often as we wanted so we practically lived there for the next nine days. One night, my father told us that the white ceiling in his room opened up, revealing a brilliant, starry sky. He also went on to tell us that he could see lush green trees. No one else could see what my father was seeing. All we could see was a white ceiling.

Over the next few days, his illness had robbed him of his ability to speak and he could only moan. He continued to do other strange things, which clearly showed that he was seeing things that none of us could see. When we spoke to the hospital staff about it, we were told that these behaviors were quite normal in the dying, especially when they came closer and closer to death.

On the final day of his life, after being bedridden for days, he suddenly got up out of bed. We struggled to keep him in bed, as he was so emaciated and sickly, and we did not want him to suffer a fall that would cause him additional pain. But he kept getting up and moaning out of frustration because we kept stopping him out of fear for his safety. He kept pointing to something we could not see and he made several attempts to go toward whatever it was. I felt so bad because a part of me wanted to honor this last wish and let him go.

That night something amazingly beautiful happened. We were sitting quietly by his bedside. I was feeling very drained, sad, and angry at his suffering, wondering if he really knew how much I loved him. I hoped that being there and praying were sufficient since I could not do anything else for him. However, it did not seem like enough. Nothing seemed good enough since he was suffering so much. I did not cry in front of him, wanting instead to show him strong compassion, but at the same time, I wondered if he knew my heart was in a million pieces. Honestly, I was going through a myriad of overwhelming emotions, feeling like I was drowning in deep despair.

Then suddenly this wave of calm and peace swept over me. I literally felt the room fill with this incredible, pure love—the biggest love anyone could ever feel. The kind of love that is so pure and big, that each time I think about it, my eyes well up with tears and I sob. That's spirit! The Godly spirit. The kind that makes you know, for certain, that everything, *absolutely* everything is going to be okay. It takes all of your fears away and restores your hope, when so badly needed. I had only felt that once before. That same wave of immense, pure love from God washed over me when Pope John Paul II went by me in his Popemobile. It's very intense and moving beyond measure.

Suddenly, the once-dim hospital room seemed to light up with this ethereal light. Then shockingly and unexpectedly, I heard my late sister clearly whisper to me, "Don't worry. Heaven is beautiful." My dad could not speak, but I know he wasn't alone. I could sense that my sister came for my father with someone else. There was more than one spirit there. They came both for him and for us, bringing us comfort in knowing that death is not the end.

 ## A Visit in the Intensive Care Unit

Dolores Reyes, Texas

My parents, a brother, and a sister of mine all passed within four years of each other from 1994 to 1997. In 2004, I ended up in the hospital with severe pancreatitis. The doctors told my boyfriend at that time that they didn't think I would make it through the night.

Looking back, I remember coming in and out of consciousness, but not being fully aware of just how sick I was. My eldest son came into the room to sign the consent for a special IV site that would be placed on my head because I was just too weak to sign anything. My other son, Ricky, visited me as well and looked so sad. People were praying for me but, again, it didn't make much sense to me.

Then the strangest thing happened. My deceased mom, dad, and sister came to visit me. They stood in the room and smiled at me and they did not walk but seemingly floated. At the time, I did not remember that they had passed away. Also, from this point on, I don't remember anyone visiting me except for my mom, dad, and sister. I was in the hospital for one month; after the third week, my doctor came to me saying, "We are going to put you back among the living." I just smiled at him, not really sure of what he meant.

Sure enough, I was moved from the intensive care unit to a regular room. My parents and my sister, again, came into the room as if to let me know that I was going to be alright. No words were spoken. On the day that I was finally going to be released my mom walked over to me and smiled. Then she waited by the door as my sister walked over to my bed. My dad was last.

When he walked over to me, however, he placed his thumb on my forehead, smiled at me, and then turned and walked over to the door to join my mom and sister. They all smiled back at me one last time and then left. I was still extremely weak and it wasn't until I got home that I realized that they were all with the Lord. Honestly, at the time, I concluded that perhaps the pain medications I was on made me hallucinate and imagine the whole thing.

A few weeks later I was feeling better and was in the kitchen teaching my son how to cook red rice. Suddenly, from the corner of my eye, I saw something very bright and white. It looked to me like a blonde-headed boy about my son's age. The bright figure had his face pressed against my bedroom door. I stared and stared in disbelief. When I finally told my son to look, the young man vanished.

Three days later, I found my 17 year old son Ricky unconscious in his room after what I thought was a seizure, as he had epilepsy. He was in full cardiac arrest and passed on July 12, 2004. Nowadays, when I look back at what happened, I think my parents and sister came to see me for a reason. They came to comfort me, but also to let me know that Ricky would be happy and safe.

I've wondered many times who the blonde-headed young man standing outside my bedroom door that day might have been. The only thing I can come up with is maybe he was looking for Ricky, as our bedroom doors are directly across from each other.

The day Ricky passed on, my other children and I came home and went into his room still numb from our loss. We just stayed in his room reminiscing and talking about the way Ricky was—how he loved everyone and was not one to judge anyone. We also talked about how he would have started his senior year of high school in just a few short weeks.

Suddenly, as we were talking about Ricky and how much we would all miss him the radio in his room went on. The radio was originally given to my mother as a gift, but when she passed away Ricky asked if he could have it. It had been broken for more than a year, but Ricky kept it as a keepsake in memory of his beloved Grandma. My mom's funeral took place on his eighth birthday and he just loved his grandmother so much.

On this night, a short time after Ricky passed, this same radio turned on all by itself. At first, I walked over and turned it off as we all continued talking. But to my astonishment, the radio went on once more and, again, I turned it off. This happened several times and I finally decided to pull the plug from the wall. I looked over at my kids, who were as amazed as I was at what was happening, and showed them that I unplugged the radio. I even laid the plug on top of the radio.

We then continued with our conversation. Shockingly, yet again, it turned on. Only this time the music was playing even louder. I grabbed the radio at this point and turned it over to check if it had a backup battery. It did not.

Without a doubt, we all knew that Ricky was with us that night. Later, when my eldest son went home, he called to tell me that dogs outside were barking and then howling. There were only two known dogs on his block but it sounded like several. This went on for about 15 minutes until my son's wife stepped outside and shouted, "Ricky, go home!" The barking then stopped immediately.

Who's There?

Margaret Kennedy, Virginia

My mom was diagnosed with a kidney disease and had other health issues, including problems with her heart. During her last year on Earth, she was in and out of the hospital.

In late October 2014, she entered the hospital for the last time. She had been there for over a week and on November 8, my father, sister, and nephew were there visiting her. My mother was intently looking straight ahead past them at the entry way. My father noticed this and asked my mother what she was looking at. In response, she said, "My mother."

My grandmother passed away in 1988. Feeling that she must have been confused, my dad said, "No, who is standing right next to you?" My sister was right next to her. My mother plainly replied, "My daughter."

She passed away the next afternoon. It was clear to my father and everyone else in the room that she was fully aware of her surroundings and in the moment.

Interestingly, she was very sick and very slow to answer whenever we asked her any questions. She was mostly in a daze due to all the toxins in her body. Yet, that day, she was very sharp. She didn't hesitate to say that her deceased mother was with them in the room. My grandmother had come to take her daughter to Heaven. This I truly believe.

Atmospheric Changes

Apparitions or spirits often interact with the environment when they appear. This can cause a wide variety of unusual incidences. Clocks have been reported to stop, alarms have sounded, and telephones have rung all at the moment of death. My sister in-law was extremely close to her Aunt Camille, who was losing her battle with cancer. One night, my brother and sister-in-law experienced a strange occurrence: The alarm sounded and the phone rang at the same time, awakening them. Soon after, they found out that Aunt Camille had just passed away.

The Art of Dying by Peter and Elizabeth Fenwick includes a story of a woman who died tragically. A short time later, her niece visited her deceased aunt's apartment and was shocked to find that every single clock had stopped at the exact moment of her death.[1]

In addition, loved ones may experience physical sensations and atmospheric changes in the room. For example, many experience a strange wind or sudden gush of air. My Uncle Tony passed away in 2003 from glioblastoma, the most common and most aggressive form of primary brain tumor. Toward the end of his two-year battle, he was unable to speak. Days before his death, he was surrounded by his daughter Maria, wife, and other family members. Without warning my uncle suddenly stared at an area in the room by the closet as he lifted his pointer finger. Everyone in the room looked in that direction, but no one was there. Suddenly, a calm breeze passed through the room as the bi-fold closet doors flew open, shocking everyone in the room. No one was near the closet and there were no windows open to explain the sudden breeze. How did the closet doors open?

My cousin Maria realized that her father stared at the same spot and asked him if someone else was in the room. She asked my uncle to lift his finger if there was someone there. In response, he obediently lifted his finger.

My Uncle Tony passed away the following week. I was extremely close to my uncle and considered him a second father. I would visit him as often as I could. When he was still able to speak, he and I shared many heartfelt conversations. Toward the end, we had one that I will never forget. He told me that his deceased mother (my paternal grandmother) had come to him. I was so surprised by his words that regrettably I didn't ask him for more information. At the time, I thought that doing so would only upset him. If I could do it all again, I would have certainly handled that situation differently. And if I had to guess, my uncle was probably pointing at my grandmother that day.

Another example of this phenomenon is the story of Bill Davis, which appeared in my book *Visits to Heaven*.[2] Davis, a Vietnam War veteran, passed away after suffering from CLL leukemia and hepatitis due to his service in the war. A few years prior to his death, he would often talk to a female spirit who appeared to him while he slept. He would even see her during his waking hours and his wife would overhear him asking, "What do you want? Why are you here?"

He told his wife that this spirit kept visiting him. In his son Bill Jr.'s words, "My dad flat-out said, 'She stands at the end of my bed and wants to take me with her.' My mom would try to trick him and talk and stand at the end of his bed but there was no fooling him. He always knew the difference, no matter how sick he was."

Days before Christmas in 2008, his father went through a procedure that would allow him to leave the hospital and spend the holidays with his family, but he knew he wouldn't survive the week. Although he hoped the procedure would work, the odds were not in his favor. During his last 36 hours, Bill was no longer able to open his eyes but was still able to hear those around him.

That Christmas ended up being a wet one, as rain covered the Northern California area for most of the day. It was an unusual day of high winds and thunder. Then suddenly during the late afternoon hours, the weather calmed, leaving no hint of wind, and a ray of sun peeked through the cloud-covered sky. Minutes later, Bill began to choke as his lungs filled with blood and water.

He then unexpectedly opened his eyes, making eye contact with everyone one at a time in the room, and started to cry, appearing afraid of what was taking place. According to his son, he held out his arms as if to block something. "I was on top of him, hugging and kissing him and holding his face. We told him it was okay and to let go. He focused his attention on my mother. They looked at each other deeply and were both crying. Then he closed his eyes and took his last breath. My mother and daughter were at his left and my wife was at the foot of the bed."

At the moment of Bill's death, his loved ones experienced an incredible phenomenon.

Within five seconds after he took his last breath, I felt something go either through me or past me. It's hard to describe. It gave me that dizzy feeling that often accompanies an amusement park or elevator ride, except this was much more powerful. My wife, mother, and daughter all felt the very same sensation. Then it became very cold in the room; there was no mistaking the change in temperature. We all experienced goose bumps and chills. It was as if the heater hadn't run all day; it was like a 15- or 20-degree drop. At that moment, my dad looked completely at peace. All the stress seemed to have left his face and he looked about 25 years younger. He even had a little grin on his face.

In another room at this same time was his daughter's boyfriend, Ryan. He had no idea that Bill Sr. had just passed. Ryan was distracted from the television and the trauma of what was happening when the double glass doors in the living room blew open without warning, as though pushed by hurricane-force winds. However, there was no wind. It was completely calm both inside and outside. Ryan got up to make his way over to the doors to close them. It was then that he felt something move through the room. At that point, he sensed someone pass by him and realized that the elder Bill must have just passed. At that moment, he said out loud, "See ya, Buddy," and closed the door.

Months later, Bill's son returned to the house to help his mother move. They were all done with the move and went back into the house to grab the last remaining box of cleaning materials. It was then that Bill Jr. became very emotional, realizing that it would be the last time he would see the house; the place held both special and difficult memories for him. It was hard to let go.

> I became very emotional and started crying. I was looking up into the sun and closed my eyes. Then out of nowhere, the same double glass doors in the living room flew open again. A small whirlwind started up on the porch kicking leaves in my face and causing me to cover my eyes. It was like a small twister or one of those dust cloud tornados. Within 15 seconds, the wind stopped. It was once again completely calm. I then turned to my mother and said, I guess he's not staying here either; he's coming with us.

His mom wholeheartedly agreed.

 ## My Mother Appeared Before My Eyes
L.A.D., Pennsylvania

My mother died in my arms. She had been suffering from rheumatoid arthritis for years, but the last eight years really took a toll on her. When she was admitted in the hospital, she couldn't walk and I knew something was really wrong. That was a Tuesday. We were told that she had a minor heart attack and also had a small fracture in her pelvis. While she was in the ER, I looked at her and told her, "Don't leave me." Her reply was, "Don't worry, Babe. I wouldn't leave you."

By Friday of that same week, she coded blue and her organs were beginning to shut down. She did not have a DNR (do not resuscitate) on file so they brought her back. At the same time this was going on, I had a weird feeling something was wrong and I left work to go straight to the hospital. Once there, the nurse told me I had to sign her up for hospice care. My mother, who raised me by herself and was the biggest influence in my life, died two days later. Everything happened so fast and I could not believe that I lost my mother in less than a week. In a matter of days, I went from being a daughter and caregiver to a 48-year old orphan. I can honestly say this was the worst time of my life.

Two days after she passed, my husband and I were sleeping on our king-sized bed with our two dogs. I was asleep for about two hours when I suddenly had a vivid dream. I say it was a dream but I know it was much more than that. I saw bright white lights going around and around. The lights kind of looked like the siren lights on a police vehicle, except these lights were bright white and very clear.

All of a sudden I heard my grandmother, who died in 1983, calling my name. Her voice woke me up and I opened my eyes to find my grandmother standing right there in front of me. She hurriedly left out of the bedroom door, however. Just as quickly as my grandmother disappeared, my mother now appeared before my eyes, except she wasn't the 78-year-old, sick woman who died in my arms. Instead she was a young, healthy woman again. She looked to be about 40 and was absolutely beautiful. As she stood there, we both looked at each other. She didn't say anything to me, but what I remember most is that she didn't look happy. She looked so sad and my feeling was that she missed me and could sense the grief that I was going through.

The entire time I could not move or talk. Normally, something like this would scare the hell out of me but it didn't. I wasn't scared at all. The experience felt like it lasted for an eternity, but it was actually only about one minute from beginning to end. My mother then just simply faded away.

My mom would continue to make her presence known during the months that followed. After she passed, I would frequently go to her house and check on things. I just wasn't ready to clean it out and let go of my childhood home. Each time I went, I could still feel her presence there. One day, I sat in her chair and was having a very bad, emotional day. I sat there having a conversation with my mother, telling her everything that was built up inside of me. I said things like "How dare you not be eating and not tell me? How dare you die in my arms? I will never be able to get that memory out of my head. How dare you keep things secret from me?" I went on and on telling her how I felt and just letting everything out.

When I was finished, I got up from her chair and said out loud, "Okay, I have to get to work." As I did this, my mother's phone began to ring. It hadn't rung in months and I was a bit startled by the ring. When I answered the phone, there was no response. What's strange is I heard something but yet it was quiet on the other end. It's hard to describe. I totally believe it was my mother letting me know that she was with me and had heard everything that I had said.

About a year after she passed, I finally decided that it was time to sell the house. I had hired some contractors to get the house ready for sale. I will never forget one worker named Tony. He told me that he could feel my mother's presence in the house. At that time, all the furniture had been removed. Yet, when Tony showed me where he sensed her, it was in the area of the living room that used to hold her recliner. This is where she always used to sit. Tony asked me for my mother's name. He wanted to talk to her as he worked on the house.

Yet another time, my 15-year-old son and I were painting the laundry room. Everything was closed upstairs and there was no one else in the house. When we were halfway done painting, we suddenly heard footsteps upstairs—my mother's footsteps. I can still see the look on my son's face. We both clearly recognized my mother's distinct footsteps.

I looked at my son and calmly told him not to worry. "We know who it is," I said, "and she would never hurt you." The house had hardwood floors so you could hear everything. And as I said, it sounded exactly like my mother's walk. It didn't faze me in the least as I was used to my mother's appearances.

I miss my mother and always will. But just as I felt her presence then, I feel her presence now. I know she's with me, just as she promised.

A Mother's Love

Carrie Sciberras, Florida

My mother went into cardiac arrest as a result of liver and kidney failure. She never recovered and had to be placed on life support. When it was determined that nothing could be done and there was no hope, my family and I heartbreakingly decided to take her off the life support machines.

Afterward, my brother, Andrew, and I kept a constant vigil in her hospital room, never leaving her side for more than a couple of minutes. I hadn't slept in a few days as I was completely obsessed with watching for any last sign of communication from my mother and savoring every last second I got to spend with her.

Death typically comes within a few hours after someone is taken off life support, but my mother's heart held on. Although she was taken off the machines on a Monday morning, she did not pass until the following Thursday. As I said earlier, my brother and I kept a constant vigil in her room, praying and watching the entire time.

I remember looking at the clock at 2 a.m. and, after that, I don't remember falling asleep. All I can say is I must have passed out from utter exhaustion because I don't at all remember laying down or even being covered up with a blanket. As it turns out, Andrew had passed out as well and was also asleep in the room. At exactly 4:30 in the morning, "something" woke me up. I don't know how I woke up or what woke me up but I do remember a feeling of peace when I opened my eyes. This feeling quickly turned to panic, however, when I suddenly realized I had fallen asleep and then frantically rushed to her side. It was obvious that she had just passed as I could still feel some warmth in her body.

At that exact moment, my husband, Manny, sent me a text asking, "Are you up?" Before answering him, I went over to Andrew to wake him up and break the news. Then I called my husband. The hospital was in Indianapolis and Manny was four hours away at home with our daughter, Aaliyah, in Illinois.

Before explaining what happened next, I have to point out that my husband and our daughter are both heavy sleepers. Once they're out, they're out until the morning. But this night was different. Manny explained that he had been woken up by Aaliyah telling him, "Grandma was just in my room. She gave me a hug."

Of course, Manny was stunned to hear that my mother had just passed away. When I later questioned Aaliyah about what happened, she told me insistently that she was sure it was Grandma. Aaliyah also noted that she was not at all scared. My mother, she said, did not say anything to her; she simply gave Aaliyah a hug and was gone.

The night my mom died was the only time during our vigil that my brother and I were both asleep. I truly believe that my mother chose to leave us when she did. She held on until both of us were asleep, knowing it would be too much for us to bear. Even in the end, she showed the unwavering power of a mother's love.

Aunt Verna

Toni DiBernardo, Pennsylvania

My Aunt Verna was very ill and staying at her daughter Mary Kay's house while she was trying to recover. She never did recover, however, and ended up passing away. For several days before she passed, Mary Kay's son kept seeing an older woman standing by the corner of the house. Bobby had no idea who she was but yet there was something familiar about her. Finally, he decided to ask his mother about this strange woman.

His mother asked for a description of the woman and was told, "She is short with gray hair and wears glasses." Mary Kay immediately went over to find a photo and brought it out for her son to see. "Is this the woman that you saw?" Bobby confirmed that it was indeed the woman in the photograph.

The woman was our deceased grandmother, Antonette. What makes this story even more amazing is that these sightings stopped as soon as Aunt Verna passed away. Was Grandma Antonette there to guide her daughter to the Other Side?

After she passed away, the family went to see a priest, who told them, "Your mother was not alone when she passed. Your grandmother went into her bedroom, took her hand, and walked her to Heaven. That's why she was by the house. She was waiting for the right time to escort her daughter home."

When the priest asked the family what kind of service they wanted, he was told that they wanted to celebrate their mother's life because she was so looking forward to seeing her family again. It was very comforting for all of us to know that Aunt Verna got her wish.

Dream Visits

A great number of deathbed visits occur during the dream state. It is much easier for those in spirit form to communicate with us while we are sleeping or in the twilight state (the period between sleeping and waking up). When we are dreaming we are between our earthly realm and the Other Side. During this time, the ego is not involved and we are more relaxed and open to receiving.

Many experience a farewell message in their dreams from someone they didn't even know passed away. And as this book has shown so far, others are suddenly awakened from sleep at the exact time a loved one crossed over.

One day while I was working on this book, my doorbell rang. It was my neighbor, Donna, who is a lab technician at a local hospital. When Donna asked what I was doing, I told her about *A Call From Heaven.* "Oh, I have a story for you," she told me anxiously. Donna went on to tell me about a friend (we'll call her Nadia), who passed away from breast cancer.

Nadia, she explained, was not one to go to the doctors for checkups and had never gone for a mammogram. When she finally did, Nadia had malignant tumors in both breasts and was already at stage four. Unfortunately, there was little hope for her and she refused chemotherapy treatment.

"Her brother visited her in the hospital and she was sleeping," Donna told me. "Suddenly Nadia woke up and clearly exclaimed, 'No, please don't go. Don't go.' Her brother was confused by her words and replied, 'I'm not going anywhere. I'm right here.' "

Nadia calmly explained, however, that she was not talking about her brother. "No, not you," Nadia said. "The angels."

Donna told me that her brother then asked her if they were good angels or bad angels. She replied, "Oh, they are all good."

"Don't worry," he told her. "If they are the good angels, they'll be back."

Two days later, Nadia passed away.

Donna went on to tell me yet another amazing story about a man who had been in a comatose state for weeks. Suddenly he sat up in bed, opened his eyes, and said his full name and his date of birth. He then lay back down, closed his eyes, and died soon after.

"It was almost like he was checking in at the gates of Heaven," Donna told me.

I'm so glad she happened to stop by that day. Her visit was a testament of just how common these deathbed phenomena are. I can think of several in my own life. One involves a special friend named Ray Skop, a faith healer from Jersey City, New Jersey.

Ray suffered a stroke on Monday, June 18, 2012. The following night, I went to bed around 2:45 a.m. and said a prayer for him. Afterward, I closed my eyes to go to sleep and immediately saw a vision of him. He looked so happy standing among luminous, beautiful green grass and trees. He looked much younger and was waving at me repeatedly saying, "Hi, Josie! Hi, Josie!"

At first, I was scared. I figured if this was really my friend then he must have crossed over and this was his way of saying goodbye to me. I also sensed a chill on the right side of my face. (It is common to experience cold spots or goose bumps when spirits are around since they use energy to communicate with us.)

Once again, I closed my eyes and for a second time I saw Ray smiling and waving at me. The third time I closed my eyes, he was gone.

Keep in mind that this happened while I was still awake. I had no doubt that what I was experiencing was real. I had no doubt that Ray's spirit was there with me. The next day I was afraid to answer the phone in fear that I would get news of my friend's passing. When the phone did ring, it was a mutual friend, who told me that Ray was still alive but in critical condition.

Ray never recovered and passed less than three weeks later, on July 3, 2012. I truly believe that Ray came to say goodbye to me that night. His body was still here but his spirit had already left.

He Has Never Let Me Down

Anna Piscitella-Musolino, Pennsylvania

I took care of my father when he was very ill. He was such a wonderful man. Although he knew he was going to die, he didn't know when. Every day that passed he would let me know how much he appreciated everything that I did for him, saying, "I know what you're doing for me and I won't forget."

At the time, I worked full time in addition to taking care of a toddler, my self-employed husband, and my sick father. After he passed away, I was lost and had many restless nights as I mourned the loss of my father. One night, my husband and I put the baby to sleep and went to bed.

All of a sudden in my sleep, I sat straight up in bed and was startled by a figure at the end of my bed. It was a man who looked to me like the Gorton's Fisherman—you know the yellow raincoat and beard. Startled, I yelled at the figure in my bedroom saying, "Hey, what are you doing in my bedroom?!" But the man only laughed, revealing himself to me. It was my father.

He then came over and sat on the side of my bed, running his hand through my hair just like he did when I was a little girl. My dad told me, "No more tears; I will help you any way that I can." He was dressed in black dress pants and a pale yellow, long-sleeved shirt. His sleeves were rolled up just like they were anytime he wore that kind of dress shirt.

It was all so real. He then went on to promise me that he would never let me down but I had to move on with my life and "no more tears." He then got up from the bed and went to my daughter's room as I followed behind him. He sat on Gianna's bed and stroked her hair just like he did mine. At that point, I was standing in my daughter's bedroom room crying. My father then looked at me and said, "Look what happens when you cry," and started to vanish.

I didn't want him to go and promised that I would try to stop the tears. He then disappeared. Somehow it seems I never left my bed and it was all part of a dream. I then found myself still sitting up in bed startled. I woke up my husband to ask him if he had seen my father. He had no idea what I was talking about.

The following morning when I woke up, I was finally at peace with my dad's passing. As crazy as this may sound, I told my husband what happened and insisted that I had to go over to the casino. For some reason, I felt my father was going to bring me some luck. I played the 5-cent slot machine and hit the jackpot of $2,500. Then I took another spin and hit the same $2,500 jackpot back-to-back. This almost never happens. Even the casino attendant couldn't believe it.

That day, I cashed out over $5,000 and was back home before my family was even out of bed. It has been over nine years since my dad passed away and to date, he has never let me down.

Author's Note: I had a feeling there was a reason Anna played the 5-cent slots and then won a total of $5,000. I wondered if the number 5 was significant. Anna confirmed that my intuition was correct; her father's birthday is December 5. Our loved ones on the Other Side are always sending us signs. This was her father's way of letting her know that it was really him.

Well, Hello, Everett!

Cindy Sheltmire, Missouri

When I was a little girl, I loved to sit on the front porch with my grandfather and read the Sunday paper. One morning, I looked at him and said, "Grandpa, do you believe in life after death?" He replied, "Nope. When you're dead, you're dead." I had faith in the afterlife even at a young age so I replied with a knowing smile, "Grandpa, you're in for a big surprise."

A few years later, my grandfather passed away. My mother told me that he had asked for a glass of milk and then suddenly looked up toward the ceiling and exclaimed in astonishment, "Well, hello, Everett!" Those were his last words.

Everett was my grandfather's brother who had died a few years before. His brother was Lewis Everett Scott, a famous major league baseball player who was also the original Iron Man. Everett had the record for the most consecutive games (1,307) until his record was later broken by Lou Gehrig and Cal Ripkin. As of this writing, he still holds the third-longest streak in history. In fact, his nickname was "Streakin' Deacon" Scott.

He played in five World Series games with the Boston Red Sox and with the New York Yankees. A shortstop, he was also close friends with Babe Ruth and roomed with him for five years. So in many ways it's not surprising that Everett was the one who greeted my grandfather and helped escort him to the Other Side.

When my mother told me about my grandfather's deathbed visit, I was so grateful to get this confirmation that he did get a big surprise at the end of his life. I can only imagine the joy he must have felt in seeing his brother again.

Author's Note: "Iron Man" was a popular term used in professional baseball to define players—mostly pitchers—who went above and beyond the normal rigors of the game. Being called an Iron Man was a compliment given only to a select group of strong players.

 ## A Message for His Wife

Cindy Sheltmire, Missouri

Cindy shared an amazing story about a visit from Heaven she received known as a "third-party sign." When this happens, those on the Other Side go to a third party to deliver a message to a loved one. It is validating to receive a message from someone who has no knowledge of what happened.

One night, I dreamed of a friend's husband, who had died a year prior. In the dream, we were in a classroom, and I was surprised to see him sitting at the desk next to mine. After class, he stood at the front of the classroom. I then went up to him, told him he looked well, and asked how he was doing. He replied that he was fine, and then he asked me if I would give a message to his wife.

I had not seen his wife since the funeral a year before. We had formerly been co-workers, but I changed companies, and we had not kept in touch. Yet I still found myself agreeing to give her the message. He said to tell her that he really liked the music. He then clearly asked, "You will give this message to my wife? You won't forget?" I promised that I would not forget, and then woke up.

At that time, I lay in bed pondering this dream, wondering if it truly was a visitation. I then decided to trust the dream to the Lord. I prayed that if this was an actual visitation, then a way would open up for me to give his wife the message. I got up and went on with my work day.

About three o'clock that afternoon, I was driving when I heard distinctly, "Don't forget to give my wife the message." Startled, I remembered the dream. I now knew I had to give his wife the message, but wondered how I was going to give her the message without spooking her. I then decided to call her office and got her secretary. I explained that I had a dream about her boss's deceased husband, and asked her to tell her boss to call me if she wanted to hear about it. That evening came and went, but I didn't hear back.

The next day, I was conducting business with clients and walked into a club house. There, to my surprise, stood the wife. Feeling that this was not a coincidence, I asked her if her secretary had given her my message. She replied that she had not gotten a message from me.

At this point I asked my clients if they could please wait in the lobby while I took his wife into another room. I then turned to the wife and told her I had a dream about her husband, and that he wanted me to tell her that he really liked the music. She burst into tears.

"Does this have meaning for you?" I asked. When she composed herself, she replied, "You might not have known this, but my husband was a musician. I tried to console myself with the hope that he liked the music in Heaven." She then told me that another friend (her pastor) also conveyed a dream message from her husband. Our loved ones who have crossed over find a way to communicate with us. Of this, I have no doubt.

 ## Ethel Mary Kates Tennis

Alice Tennis, Hawaii

Raised in Manhasset, New York, I was blessed to have a blissfully happy childhood and loving parents. Eventually, we moved to Honolulu, Hawaii, in 1970 and lived a content life—something that had always been my father's dream.

Dad passed away from a massive heart attack years later in 1982. Eventually, my mom became ill and was living in an assisted living facility in Florida. She wasn't happy there, however. So my sister Janet and I brought her back to Hawaii, and I became her caretaker.

Just to give you an idea of just how wonderful she was, my mother was a World War II Navy WAVE Veteran. She had a lovely voice and sang for the troops with Tex Beneke of the Glenn Miller Orchestra. Admiral Byrd once picked her up in his white chauffeur-driven limo as she was waiting for the bus on base. He talked to Mom at length about her home life in New York and her experience in the Navy. She led a full, productive life and her mind was extremely sound until the end.

My mother experienced a myriad of mystical experiences over the years. So many, in fact, that I started to keep a journal of her experiences. For example, there were angelic visitations in her room. She also told of receiving telepathic messages from the Other Side as well as having lucid dreams of the Heavenly realms.

She passed away on April 25, 2011, at the age of 91. As I remember that day, I know for certain that she did not die alone. At the time, we lived in what is known as an old plantation home by the old Waialua Sugar Mill on Oahu's North Shore. I was in the kitchen preparing breakfast and what would be my mother's last meal. I made a simple fried egg and buttered toast with a small cup of coffee.

From the kitchen, I could still see my mother in her bedroom. She was sitting upright toward one corner of her bedroom in the direction of her flat screen TV. Mom called out aloud, "Everett! Everett! Everett!"

This was followed by, "Peggy! Peggy! Peggy!" She then yelled out, "Mary! Mary! Mary!" It was very clear to me that my mother was seeing them in the room. Everett was her older brother and Peggy was her sister-in-law. Peggy was married to my mom's brother, Jim. Both Everett and Peggy had recently passed.

I wasn't sure who my mother was referring to when she mentioned Mary. My mom did have an Aunt Mary so I asked her if this was who she was referring to. But my mother surprised me when she said, "No, the Blessed Mother Mary!"

I am certain that they all came to comfort her and take her home. My mother fell in and out of a coma-like sleep and then quietly exhaled her last breath around noon the following day.

 ## A Joyous Musical Reunion

Jennifer Carter, New Jersey, www.thesearchforlifeafterdeath.com

I held my grandmother's hand as she lay dying in the hospital, keeping a watchful eye as she rested. All the while, I couldn't help but think of my last visit with her and how disturbed she had been. Although she seemed otherwise lucid, my grandmother had claimed that something or someone was visiting her in the middle of the night, trying to steal her away. She struggled to describe these beings to me and seemed unconvinced of what she saw. Eventually she settled on describing them as aliens, which at the time I simply discounted as hallucinations due to the use of medications.

These visions weren't at all comforting to her, and in her paranoia she even claimed that the hospital staff was trying to kill her. This was a worrying statement, but there was no proof that she wasn't getting good care, and we attributed these statements to the stress of being in the hospital.

On this day, however, her demeanor was completely different. My grandmother, whom I called "Oma," was peaceful and resting comfortably. As I sat and held her hand patiently waiting for a whispered word, a smile came to her lips. She opened her eyes and turned toward me with a face full of wonder and disbelief.

"They were here last night," she said. "They came to see me."

"Who, Oma?" I asked. "The doctors?"

"No," she said wonderingly, her voice lowering to barely a whisper, "my father . . . and my brother. They were here, singing and reading poetry to me."

She smiled broadly and relaxed back into her pillow, deeply satisfied. Although her father had died nearly 60 years before, and her brother at least a decade prior, I didn't have the heart to question her experience. I simply patted her hand and declared how wonderful it was that they came to visit, to which she emphatically agreed. I left my grandmother's hospital room that day relieved that whatever had transpired left her in complete peace and contentment. I would never see her alive again; she died very soon after my visit.

Years later, I learned about the miracle of deathbed visions and most of the pieces fell into place. Although most deathbed visions are comforting to the dying, some may initially be misinterpreted or confusing. Combined with the stress of hospitalization, I now believe she initially feared these visions. Only the appearance of her family could have provided the comfort and security she needed to let go of life and pass into the next world.

But one question lingered in my mind: Why hadn't my grandmother been visited by her own mother, whom she had cared for in her own home for most of her life? After learning more about my grandmother's life, the answer became clear.

My grandmother idolized her musically inclined father, who sung in a barbershop quartet. My grandmother inherited his musical talent, excelling at the piano. She became very close to her father, sharing this special musical connection. When her beloved father died unexpectedly, she was devastated. As a young woman, she now had the sole responsibility for caring for her rather dismissive and distant mother, who had always instead favored her handsome and popular son, Jack. My grandmother faded into the role of caretaker and housekeeper, overshadowed by her brother's achievements. Jack was the football star, then later the successful businessman, and finally the state senator. Although my grandmother dutifully cared for her mother throughout her convalescence, she never received the affection or approval her mother lavished on her son. Despite her likely disappointment, my grandmother always spoke of her brother with great pride.

My grandmother's visitation now made perfect sense. A visitation from her mother may have been too distressing for my grandmother who more than likely was not emotionally ready for reconciliation. However, the unexpected reappearance of her beloved father and brother made her feel special and cherished and ready for her joyous spiritual reunion.

Although I could not directly share in her experience at the time, I know now that my grandmother received a final blessing that could only have come from Heaven. Her family welcomed her into a state of peace, offering her a kind of solace that eased her passing. Comforted by the music she and her father shared in her childhood, I believe my grandmother stepped into the light feeling completely safe and loved;

her life was finally celebrated not for what was created with earthly hands, but for all that she cultivated with her heart.

Yellow Roses for Nancy

One of our four metaphysical senses, clairaudience is the gift of clear hearing, which is often compared to having a mental inner ear. People who have the gift of clairaudience can receive messages in thought form from spirit guides, deceased loves ones, and so on. These are the thoughts that pop into your head without you consciously thinking them.

Those on the Other Side are very capable of communicating with us and do so all the time. They may even enlist the help of others to get a message to a loved one or even deliver a gift. Last week, a man I had never met used me to deliver a special surprise to his wife, Nancy.

I was home recovering from a medical procedure; since I was laid up and needed to rest, I took the time to read my friend Nancy Clark's book, *Divine Moments: Ordinary People Having Spiritually Transformative Experiences.* By the second day, I quickly came to the last chapter. In it, Nancy talks about the loss of her husband, Ched. She tells readers how she loves yellow roses and how her husband would always give her yellow roses on special occasions.

As I read the last three lines, "There is one thing I know for sure. Love never dies. LOVE NEVER DIES!" I smiled to myself knowing the truth of those very words and closed the book. Just as I did, I heard a voice in my head say, "Buy Nancy yellow roses." At first, I was stunned. I wondered, *Buy Nancy yellow roses?* This must be Nancy's husband, Ched.

My husband was working from home so I immediately told him what happened and he replied that I should send the roses if I really felt that the message was from Nancy's husband. I sent Nancy an email asking for her address, saying that I would explain later. A short time later, Nancy replied, but she did not include her address. Instead, she said something that stunned me: She wrote how much she missed her husband, adding, "This Saturday we would have celebrated our 50th wedding anniversary. We were going to renew our vows."

This was all the confirmation I needed. Now I understood why Ched wanted me to send Nancy the roses. I emailed Nancy again, asking her to please send me her address. This time she did reply with her address and I went online searching for the perfect yellow roses. I saw a bouquet of yellow roses and lilies. I thought this was a beautiful combination since I like lilies. But when I went to order the flowers, I kept getting an error message. It kept telling me that my security code was invalid. I had the feeling that these were not the roses Ched wanted for his wife. So I went back to a different bouquet with 14 long-stem premium yellow roses. I used the same credit card and put in the same security code. No problem. It worked.

I then arranged for the roses to arrive on Saturday, April 28th, which would have been Nancy and Ched's 50th wedding anniversary. The following is an account of what happened that day in Nancy's own words.

I have been praying all year for a sign from Ched, something that would let me know he is still aware of my love for him and that he is near. I prayed that Ched would bring me a sign for our anniversary date today.

The following is the answer to my prayers. I have a dear friend in New Jersey who I never met but I love her very much. Her name is Josie Varga. She is an author like myself who is interested in sharing the good news about after-death communications and life beyond death.

Just a few days ago, Josie emailed me and asked me what my address was as she was going to send me something. She gave no hint what she was going to send, but I gave her my address without hesitation. After I gave her my address, I mentioned that April 28th would be my 50th wedding anniversary.

The big day arrives today. I am praying for a sign from Ched on this very emotional day for me. I browse through our wedding album and cry a lot because I miss him so much. A hole in my heart is as large as the city I live in. Yet, I know he is okay. I know he is filled with love, joy, and peace unspeakable, yet it does not soothe the raw emotion of pain that separation has created. I ache to receive a message from him today, but what kind of message, I have no idea. I would leave that up to the mysterious universe. But the day is coming to a close. It is 5 p.m. already and nothing has happened.

Knock, knock. Someone is at the front door. I have a lung virus for weeks now and I look like a distressed haggard, but I answer the door. A young man in a suit is carrying an arrangement of 14 beautiful long-stemmed YELLOW ROSES in a vase of water! He hands the arrangement to me and wishes me a happy anniversary. I'm anxious to see who sent these beautiful yellow roses to me so I quickly read the card. It says: "Dear Nancy, these roses are not from me; they are from Ched. Happy Anniversary with all his love. I heard a voice telling me to buy you yellow roses. Please call me and I will explain. Love you, Josie."

I broke down sobbing from happiness that filled every crevice of my heart. I immediately called Josie and she explained that one day she heard a voice in her head telling her to buy Nancy yellow roses. She said it stunned her. "Why?" she wondered. She had no idea why she was supposed to buy me yellow roses! She told her husband about the voice in her head telling her to "buy Nancy some yellow roses" but didn't understand why she should do this. She asked her husband what she should do. He told her to go ahead and buy them. So the next thing Josie did was email me and ask me what my address was. She didn't tell me why she wanted it and I didn't ask. The story played out fully today when the yellow roses arrived at my doorstep.

Remember, Ched contacted Josie to tell her to buy me yellow roses BEFORE she knew my anniversary was coming up in a few days. She listened to that voice in her head and made a decision to buy them for me without knowing why. Only after she asked me for my address did I tell her that my anniversary was coming up in a few days. I can imagine how Josie must have felt when she learned about my upcoming anniversary and then to know that Ched's spirit contacted her to send me the yellow roses. She must have been overjoyed to be an instrument of love from Ched to me.

It is 45 degrees outside today, rainy, and cold. Even though I have had a bad virus for three weeks, I donned a warm coat and took one long-stemmed yellow rose from the arrangement Josie sent; I took Ched's photo, my heart-shaped necklace that contains some of Ched's ashes, his wedding ring, my Bible, and a new ring that I would use to renew my vow to love him for eternity. I walked to the memorial garden I created for him where some of his ashes remain and I sat on the bench near him. The wind whistled through the tall ash trees and the chilly mist perched on my eyeglasses but I was warmed by the love I was feeling for Ched and for the sign he brought me on this anniversary day to let me know his love is still with me.

Before I left, I thanked God for the amazing gift I received today, knowing that love never dies and that even in death there is a way for our loved ones to touch our lives in a way that defies understanding. The universe is filled with love and when we tap into it, we become transformed by it. I know that happened to me today.

I share this story in the hopes that all who read it will know that nothing will ever break the bond of love between two souls. Love is the only thing that matters now and it is the only thing that we will take with us when we leave this earthly realm. Love is all that is.

Words cannot describe the sheer joy I felt in my heart when I realized that Nancy's husband was using me as an instrument to express his eternal love for his wife. I am both humbled and honored. I end this heartwarming story with Nancy's words: "The moral of this story is that love never dies. Love between souls who shared a physical life together continues to exist after death. The mystery of the afterlife cannot be understood, only welcomed into the sacredness of the human heart where it can continue to nourish and instill the peace that passeth all understanding."

Final Gifts

Dr. Betty Phillips

Dr. Betty Phillips has helped therapy clients for more than 30 years, earning her PhD in psychology from Harvard University. She has been recognized for her extensive community service and was honored as Psychologist of the Year by the Austin Capital Area Psychological Association. This is her story about her father's deathbed visit.

Worried, I called my father's doctor. "My father is saying things that don't make any sense. Do you think it's his medication?" My very elderly father, now living with my family, had been admitted to home hospice care a while earlier. He was only on one medication, but I felt I needed to contact the doctor to discuss the possibility of a medication reaction. Nevertheless, what my father was saying was very interesting: My mother had contacted him to say she was waiting for him at home. And he needed to buy a ticket home.

My mother died six years ago and their home in Florida had been sold. My father knew this, but he had almost been in a trance during this talk about buying tickets home. My father's doctor reassured me that it was not the medicine and referred me to a book about deathbed visits, entitled *Final Gifts*, written by experienced hospice nurses

Maggie Callanan and Patricia Kelley. The book was a gift to me and will be to you if you are not familiar with the needs of a dying individual. Most of us are not!

The transition from a dying body to the return to eternal life is often difficult and frightening to the dying individual and his or her family members. Even more frightening is the problem created when the dying are unable to communicate their needs and family members dismiss their communications as confused thinking. Callanan and Kelley describe a mindset they term "nearing death awareness," which develops slowly as a dying individual drifts between life and the return to eternal life. This period can last for days, weeks, or even months, and is different from the deathbed visions that often occur at the moment of death.

Admit it: We're scared about our own mortality, and most of us prefer to avoid the topic of death, usually assigning it to doctors and hospitals. But let's not avoid our loved ones as they begin the transition from this life to the return to eternal life. The experience is actually awesome and empowering (yes, and also stressful as we extend out of our comfort zone). The information from near-death experiences, deathbed visions, and afterlife encounters tells us that the actual time of death, the transition time, can be experienced as a peaceful and comforting experience, bathed in a white light, full of love and understanding, with deceased family members and friends coming to escort the dying individual into eternal life. To facilitate this peaceful transition we can give our loved ones the "final gift" of acceptance, love, and hope during this last period of time, whether that is hours, days, or months. The dying give us a final gift when they reach out to communicate with us.

During the nearing-death awareness period, our dying family members are often able to talk and they do communicate their needs, but sometimes in indirect, symbolic, or confusing ways. Dying individuals often speak of tickets home. The metaphor of the journey generally relates to the dying experience and home is their final destination.

The dying often tell us they are in the presence of loved ones who have already passed on. It's important not to be frightened by such stories and it's equally important to accept their stories. Sometimes they tell us about their visions of the afterlife, or sometimes they tell us things they need to do before they die, such as reconcile with others. In other cases, dying people communicate without words, and their actions show us what they are experiencing. They may nod, smile, wave, or reach for someone you cannot see. My father often talked aloud with my mother as he lay in his bed. He knew that she had died, but he was equally convinced that she was there with him. He would often start to whisper if I walked past the open door of his bedroom. Somehow I also knew she was there and had told him to keep their conversation private!

My father passed away in 2007 and I have been pursuing the topic of the survival of consciousness ever since. I was trained as a scientist with a doctorate in psychology, but I found I had much to learn. Pierre Teilhard de Chardin once said, "We are not human beings on a spiritual journey. We are spiritual beings on a human journey." Are we? Spiritual and religious writers have provided a great deal of information in these areas. An impressive body of knowledge is being accumulated, although the topic remains controversial to some.

I'll mention quantum physics briefly because it provides a basis for understanding our energetic or spiritual foundations. Although the material world looks solid and stable to us, we now know it is composed of energy vibrating in different frequencies out of concordance with time and space laws of the observable world. As energy does not disappear, what happens to the energy in our body when we die? The next question is whether this energy is consciousness and whether it is or has been localized in the brain. The consciousness that appears to survive death is often described as the soul. But can or will hard science validate these experiences?

Dr. Sam Parnia has been conducting studies of near-death experiences after cardiac arrest in which the mind and body are flat-lined yet the patients report an NDE if they are able to be resuscitated.

Specifically, Dr. Parnia is attempting to find out whether consciousness persists after the brain is effectively dead, showing that the location of consciousness, otherwise called the soul, will continue to function without the brain. You may have heard that the NDE is just a hallucination produced by a dying brain probably due to drugs or lack of oxygen. Dr. Parnia has already ruled out both explanations and is continuing with rigorously designed double-blind trials of patients after cardiac arrest.

When the time came for my father's transition, he had some blissful experiences, seeing wonderful colors and flowers as well as my mother and his friends coming to help him on his new journey. My father's death is what led me on my quest for spiritual knowledge and actually transformed me from a nonbeliever to a believer. Earlier I had asked him to send me a sign to let me know when he got to Heaven. About a half hour after his transition, owls appeared outside his window. I had gotten my sign. And that was the first of many I've received from my father and my family in spirit.

For more information on Dr. Betty Phillips visit *www.bettyphillipspsychology.com.*

Spiritual but Not Religious

As mentioned earlier, renowned researcher Raymond Moody, MD, has spent more than 40 years studying the afterlife and what happens when we die. When Dr. Moody first began researching the near-death experience, there was almost no literature from which to base his research. Since coining the phrase *near-death experience* (NDE) in the late 1970s he has written 12 books. Two of those, *Life After Life* and *Reunions,* have sold more than 13 million copies worldwide.

Through the years, he has done countless interviews and has investigated thousands of near-death experiences. In August 1988, he

sat down with Jeffrey Mishlove, PhD, the host of *Thinking Allowed.*
Jeffrey is a licensed clinical psychologist and author who has served as
president of the Intuition Network. When questioned in his interview
about whether such experiences seem to suggest there is an afterlife
or a "world beyond," Moody noted that he had spoken with more than
a thousand people who claimed to have had an NDE. As a result, he
stated that he did not mind admitting that the "really baffling and
unusual features" of these reported experiences gave him the self-
assurance and confidence he needed to believe in life after death.

Dr. Moody also told Mishlove that based on what his patients told
him he could honestly say he had no doubt whatsoever that "they did
get a glimpse of the beyond."[1]

Much has certainly changed since Dr. Moody's interview with
Thinking Allowed. More people are willing to share such spiritual
phenomena than ever before; this book is certainly a testament to
that fact. Of course, not everyone was willing to share publicly. Some
told me their stories privately and others wanted only their first names
revealed, but the majority was more than happy and willing to share
their deathbed visits.

However, some things remain unchanged. Dr. Moody, for example, spoke of how those who have such experiences often describe
themselves as spiritual but not necessarily religious. In a 2012 survey
by the Pew Religion and Public Life Project nearly 37 percent of
those who said they were not religiously affiliated considered themselves spiritual but not religious (SBNR).[2] Although you'll find many
differing opinions, SBNR generally means that the person doesn't
follow organized or church religion yet still believes in a higher spiritual source.

Perhaps this is because more and more studies are being conducted on the metaphysical than ever before or because so many
stories are being made public in books, films, and so on. Renowned
mystic Edgar Cayce once said, "As we approach the Golden Age, the

veils shall be removed and the people of the Earth shall become aware of the people of the Universe." Cayce's prediction can certainly be seen in the world around us as more and more seek spiritual growth and awareness.

When asked about the effects of such experiences, Dr. Moody explained that those who had a near-death experience claim that they are no longer are afraid of dying. This doesn't mean, however, that they would want to die or that they are not grateful for the life they have been given.

Such experiences actually magnify one's feelings of gratitude, according to Moody. They don't want to die anytime soon because they say that life is an immense blessing and a wonderful opportunity to learn, "but what they mean is that when death comes in its natural course of events, they're not going to be afraid. They don't fear it in the least anymore as being a cessation of consciousness."[3]

David Kessler, a well-known expert and author on death, grief, and healing, would surely agree. His most recent book was written with Louise Hay and two others were co-written with the legendary Elizabeth Kubler-Ross. His work was praised by the late Mother Teresa and his services have been used by many celebrities including Jamie Lee Curtis and the late Elizabeth Taylor.

Kessler's best-selling book, *Visions, Trips, and Crowded Rooms*, highlights many amazing stories from the bedsides of the dying to enlighten and inspire those of us left behind. Throughout his research and his many years of working with the dying, Kessler found that those on their deathbed are most often greeted by their deceased mother or a mother-figure. This finding, he notes, should not come as a surprise since the person who was there for you when you came into this life and raised you would surely want to be there as you took your last breath.[4]

Kessler also noted that he has never come across anyone who claimed to have a deathbed visit or experience outside of their realm of faith. He has never come across a Muslim who claimed to be greeted by Jesus or a Christian who claimed to be greeted by Allah. However, he does note that the belief in angels appears to cross all religious boundaries, as people of all faiths have claimed to see these celestial beings on their deathbed. In addition to being greeted by a mother-figure and seeing angels, Kessler found that the dying often reach upward, say they are going on a trip, and speak of being in a crowded room.[5]

Kessler makes a convincing point in concluding his book: Some insist that people are so desperate for an afterlife that they invent it.

> Those who say that there is nothing when we die have faith, too. They just have faith that there is nothing. I'm not sure who told them that or where they got their information, but I do know that the dying don't say, "Here comes nothing. I now see nothing." And health-care professionals don't report that the dying speak of entering a "nothingness." I'm going to believe the words of the dying over the beliefs and doubts of the living who haven't lost a loved one or worked in a hospital or hospice setting.[6]

It's interesting to note that the last words of the dying are considered believable or trustworthy under the law. In *People vs. Clay* (decided June 28, 2011), two men were convicted of murder when a police officer testified in court to statements made by a dying victim. The rationale is that the dying person would have no reason to lie or fabricate his or her story. I would argue the same for those who claim to have these deathbed experiences. They have no reason to lie and every reason to tell the truth.

NDEs in Terminally Ill Patients Differ From Those in Acute Events

Dr. Pamela M. Kircher

A family doctor and hospice/palliative care physician, Dr. Pamela Kircher is also an author and international speaker on end-of-life issues and near-death experiences. The following chapter appeared in her book Love is the Link: A Hospice Doctor Shares Her Experience of Near Death and Dying.

From talking with people who have had NDEs in all kinds of situations, I've come to some conclusions as to how NDEs in terminally ill patients differ from those that occur in acute situations. First, the episodes in terminally ill patients do not necessarily come at times of severe physiologic compromise as they do in people with acute NDEs. Second, seeing dead relatives is much more common in terminally ill patients than in people with acute NDEs. Third, a life review is more common in acute NDEs than in NDEs of hospice patients. Fourth, the purpose of the NDE in acute situations appears to be to help the person learn to live in more loving ways, whereas the purpose of an NDE in terminally ill people seems to be to help them die in peace.

It is extremely common for terminally ill patients to have an NDE in the last few days of life, and it may not necessarily occur at a time of severe physiologic compromise. On several occasions, I have entered the room of a patient who was clearly conversing with someone that I was not seeing. If a family member was in the room, it was usually reported that this had been going on for some time. Unlike a patient who is having hallucinations, these patients will answer my questions coherently. After answering the questions, they will return to what they were doing before I entered the room and interrupted their important communication process with spirits I wasn't able to see. It is not unusual for them to share that communication with me and/or relatives either a few hours later or the next day.

These conversations have usually taken place with a deceased relative, but some people have told me that they were talking with a religious figure, usually Jesus, or even with a completely unknown figure (although that is much less common). My experience is that many more terminally ill patients visit with deceased relatives than people who have an NDE under acute conditions. Generally speaking, it is extremely helpful to the dying person to communicate with these deceased relatives.

One elderly man whose wife had died of Alzheimer's disease two years before he contracted terminal cancer was delighted when he "visited" with her in her pre-Alzheimer state. He exclaimed that he "got my wife back!" They had been wonderful companions to each other for some 50 years before the Alzheimer's disease took her away from him long before her death. He had cared for her for the last several years of her life, and it was very painful for him to see the person that he knew slip away while her body remained.

After the "visitation" experience, he believed that he would be reunited with his beloved wife in her pre-Alzheimer condition. That belief allowed him to approach the last few days of his life with equanimity, and even a measure of joy.

An encounter with Jesus made all the difference to another hospice patient. She was a very angry woman in her 40s, who was devoted to her family of several children, most of whom were still at home when she got cancer. As her body began to be overcome by the cancer, she steadfastly refused to talk about her terminal illness to anyone, including her husband. She vehemently insisted that she was too young to die and that it simply wasn't going to happen. She was not finished yet and she didn't want to talk further about it.

Her pain was difficult to manage because emotional pain and anger intensify the physical pain of terminal cancer. In spite of multiple medication adjustments and multiple visits from the social worker and the chaplain, some pain remained, in large part due to her distressing emotional condition. When I prayed about ways to assist her in her pain, I got the clear feeling that she would be helped, but not in the usual ways that our patients were helped. Two days later, she had a profound mystical experience that completely changed her attitude toward life and her impending death.

In her mystical experience, she found herself in a beautiful meadow with her mother, who looked young and healthy even though she had died several years before. She assured her that she would be with her and that she would be in a calm and peaceful place. She found herself relaxing and re-experiencing the love that she had felt for her mother. As she turned to the side, she saw Jesus with his arms outstretched and a loving expression on his face. The woman felt a strong pull toward Jesus. However, she remembered her family at home and realized that she had not yet told them goodbye. She told Jesus that she was not yet ready to come, but that she would soon be ready. With that declaration, she found herself back in her body in her bed at home.

Throughout the next two days, one by one the children were called in privately to her bedroom where she told them how much she loved them and that she would be watching over them in her death just the way that she had in her life. She spent time with her husband, helping him to prepare for her death and single parenting. When she had done what she could to prepare them, she said that she was ready to go. Within a few hours she became unresponsive and then died peacefully the next day. The grieving process was much easier for her family because of her experience than it would have been had she died in confusion and anger, denying her imminent death.

NDEs in terminally ill patients do seem to have the purpose of helping them to prepare for death. Although people often find it very useful to spend a great deal of time in the last weeks and months of life contemplating their lives and trying to make peace in areas where forgiveness is needed, they rarely tell me about life reviews in their NDEs. In contrast, life reviews are fairly common in people with acute NDEs.

One person with an acute NDE, for example, told me that he "saw" every event that had occurred in his life, including the times that he was extremely unkind. The feeling he drew from the Being of Light who watched his life review with him was that it was all perfect, even the "mistakes." It was all part of the lessons that he came here to learn. Because of this life review, he revised his understanding of the meaning of life. Prior to the experience, he had seen life as a series of random events that occur until death ends it all. Because of the experience, he realized that life has meaning and that it is important to learn to be loving. Furthermore, the experience convinced him that there is more to life than just this life on Earth. As a result of the experience, he believes that the spirit goes on beyond this life.

A similar change in perspective occurred in a hospice patient, although she didn't have a life review. This lady was an atheist and extremely angry about dying young, when she had barely begun to live. Her husband held similar views. As the patient became less and less responsive, her husband sat by her side in intense anger and grief.

When the patient had been unresponsive for two days, she suddenly awakened to tell her husband of a remarkable experience. She found herself going down a tunnel that was frightening at first because of the sense of lack of control and the speed of the traveling. However, she began to be attracted to a bright light at the end of the tunnel. To her amazement, as she approached the light, she felt surrounded by an incredible feeling of peace and love and she saw Jesus with his arms outstretched. Her tension, anger, and pain melted away. She felt that she had a choice about staying, but she wanted to tell her husband about the experience since it was so helpful and so different than what they had both believed about death. With the decision made, she found herself back in her body struggling toward consciousness to share her story.

After sharing this story, she became peacefully unresponsive and died a day or two later in peace. Needless to say, that shared experience was enormously helpful to her husband in the grieving process. Learning how to live life had not been as important to the hospice patient as learning how to die peacefully; perhaps that is why she didn't undergo a life review.

Sometimes the encounters in NDEs of terminally ill patients are more mysterious. One man who was quite clear-headed, for example, kept seeing a small child in the room during the last couple weeks of his life. As far as he could remember, this was no one that he knew. They never said anything to each other. The child was simply silently present: He would sit or stand and not move about at all, and he had a peaceful energy about him. The man told his wife about the child because it was so puzzling. We never did understand the significance of the silent witness. In addition to the strange child in the corner of the room, this same man frequently "saw" dead relatives throughout the last several days of his life. In fact, his wife said that he seemed to be in that world more often than he was in this one those last several days. I've often wondered if he discovered the identity of that mysterious child after his death.

Most terminally ill patients who have NDEs encounter dead relatives. In contrast, visits with dead relatives occur only occasionally in acute NDEs. One young woman shared with me an NDE that occurred to her during a surgery that went awry. She met a soldier who introduced himself as her grandfather, Samuel. She had never met her grandfather, as he had died in his 40s before she was born. Her "visiting" grandfather said that he wanted to tell her how sorry he was that he had been unable to demonstrate love to his son (her father) and he understood that was why his son was unable to demonstrate love to her. He went on to say that if there was one thing that he could have changed about his life that would have been the thing. When she recovered from the anesthesia, she asked her father about her grandfather. In all her years, he had never even mentioned his father's name to her before. He said that his name was Samuel, and that he didn't want to talk about him. Later, in a drawer, she found a picture of a young soldier who looked just like the Grandfather Samuel that she met in her NDE.

She said that the experience was extremely helpful to her in learning how to be understanding toward her own father's difficulty expressing affection. She credited that experience with helping her get through her teen years with this very controlling father. Even though her experience was with a dead relative, its purpose was clearly to help her live her life with more understanding, not prepare for her death.

Another case involved a little boy who had cancer. By the time that he was terminally ill at 2 years old, he had spent more than half of his life in hospitals with chemotherapy and complications of the illness. He was a frail little boy who appeared wise beyond his years, although he could say only a few words because of his young age. During the two days before his death, his mother and grandmother both witnessed him on at least two occasions having what seemed to be an NDE in his crib. When they watched him from the doorway of his bedroom (where he couldn't see them), they saw him stand up in the corner of his crib and lift his arms up to an unseen figure. At those times, he seemed to glow and had a beautiful smile on his face. No one was in the room except for the little boy and his "angel." He died peacefully a day later with a beautiful smile on his face. That radiant death was a real source of comfort to his family, who had watched their tiny son suffer so much in his short life. They felt comforted to know that he was finally in a safe place and no longer in pain.

These experiences happen at all stages of life. One woman told me about the profound changes that her husband underwent when he had an NDE one week before his death from cancer. He declared to her that he had "seen the face of God" while being surrounded by light. Although he had never been particularly religious, he now declared that he knew beyond a shadow of a doubt that there was a God and that he wanted to go right then. He insisted that all of the tubes (IVs, etc.) be removed, and then he relaxed. To his chagrin, he lived another week—not particularly in physical discomfort, but in impatience. His NDE spawned a deep interest in mysticism in his wife, a passion that she is still pursuing some 20 years after his death. In that way, his NDE made a very profound difference in her life.

Volunteers are particularly aware of these aspects for several reasons. First, they have the time to be aware. Unlike the staff, who are busying themselves with the details of patient care, the volunteers' sole purpose is just to "be there." Second, they do not have the emotional load that the family has. The family is attentive to the dying patient, of course, but much of their attention is drawn to their own pain, uncertainty, and anger. Third, people drawn to hospice work are particularly sensitive and spiritual; they are likely to be aware of very real energy shifts that other people just don't notice because of lack of sensitivity.

One male volunteer shared the story of his first hospice patient. He visited a young man, who was dying of AIDS, in his home on several occasions during the last few months of his life. During those visits, he came to view him as a wonderful friend and teacher. As the patient came closer to death, he allowed the volunteer to share his internal processes as he gradually shifted from a physical being to an entirely spiritual one. In the final few days, they experienced times when the patient did not seem to have a physical body at all; his limbs felt as if "they were water." The volunteer felt as though he could pass his hands through the patient's arms in those times when he hovered between this plane and the next one. When he made his transition, the volunteer was there to hear the patient say "It's beautiful!" as he died with a beatific smile. I feel that he was able to do that easy transition through the last few days because he had resolved his issues in this lifetime and was, therefore, able to focus on his transition process.

A young male volunteer told of being with a patient shortly after he died. While waiting for the patient's family to arrive, the volunteer was dozing on the window seat when he felt a breeze go by that raised the hairs on his arm. It felt to him that the spirit of the deceased person was blowing by.

Pausing to fully participate in life and death may well be the main message of hospice work and NDEs. We miss so much of what life is most about when we are so busy doing that we do not take time to be. When we are in a mode of being, we are open to subtle energies and profound experiences. When we are in a mode of rapid doing, we are closed to the profound moments of life unless we are slammed into an NDE by a car accident or a heart attack! Terminally ill people who have NDEs are usually more in a mode of being and, hence, they frequently come and go between both worlds.

After talking with hundreds of people in the past several years, I am convinced that contact with alternate realities is the rule rather than the exception. Nearly everyone has multiple opportunities to live from these experiences whether they choose to or not. The chief barrier to this is that people doubt their own experiences and, if they do believe them, they are reluctant to share them with others for fear of being ridiculed.

Through the years, people have said to me hundreds of times, "I haven't said this to anyone else, but can I tell you about this 'weird' experience?" Yes, sometimes this occurs after a talk or after someone has read my book, but it also happens in airports with total strangers who simply sense my energy as someone who will listen to their experiences with an open mind.

If we would dare to tell our truths and dare to listen openly and deeply to one another, the awareness of what truly moves us would expand exponentially overnight.

For more information about Dr. Pamela M. Kircher, visit *www.pamkircher.com.*

FINAL THOUGHTS

The manner in which we live our lives, to a large extent, depends on what we believe comes after it.

—Chris Carter

Death will always carry with it a certain mystical component. No one can truly know what happens when we die; however, these deathbed visits and other metaphysical phenomena certainly do provide a confirming hint of what lies beyond this world.

People always ask me if dealing with the death of a loved one is easier for me now that I know there is an afterlife. My answer is always the same: It's easier, but not easy. Dealing with the death of a loved one is never easy. It hurts—it really hurts. But yet I find comfort in the knowledge that life does continue. I find comfort in knowing love truly never dies and that I will see my loved ones again.

When a loved one dies, I am saddened by the fact that I can't see them whenever I want, and can no longer feel them and hug them. But I don't think of it as the end of the relationship. It's not the end of all communication; it is only the start of a different form of communication: spirit.

Another question that I am often asked is whether or not I am afraid to die. In order to answer this question honestly, I have to respond with, "No, I am not afraid to die, but yes, I am afraid of how I am going to die." In my opinion, there is no need to fear something that isn't really going to happen. Yes, we die physically but we are still very much alive spiritually.

Loss of fear is a universal consequence for those of us who have either had or witnessed such spiritually transformative experiences (STEs) as deathbed visits. But what about those who have not had such an experience?

"If we have never had a transcendental existence we can only theorize about what a transcendental existence might be like, or indeed whether it is more than a theoretical possibility," writes Dr. Peter Fenwick in *The Art of Dying.* "But perhaps we can learn more by listening to the people who have first-hand knowledge of the experiences the rest of us can only talk about."[1]

Dr. Peter Fenwick, a respected neuropsychiatrist and world-renowned expert on near-death and deathbed phenomena, points out that these experiences seem to lead to tranquility in the face of death not only for the dying, but also for the family and friends who witness them.

> To complete our jigsaw we will need to expand our current scientific framework, and hope that this may provide an explanation. But it's also important to realize that these experiences have their own validity, that in their powerful emotional and spiritual impact they have meaning for us, and only those who have had the experiences are entitled to judge their personal meaning. These experiences leave a strong and marked impression on those who grieve and are a source of comfort over the years that follow.[2]

Experiencing such phenomena, however, does far more than bring us comfort and take away the fear of death. It also changes your view of life. Once we come to understand that life does continue, we also come to realize that we are far more than the physical body. Our true essence is not the body. Our true essence is spirit.

Renowned astronomer and scientist Carl Sagan is known for his popular quote "Extraordinary claims require extraordinary evidence." On the surface, it's a self-explanatory statement. If you make an extraordinary claim, you better have evidence to back it up. But what is extraordinary to some may not be extraordinary to others. The reason for this is because of our presuppositions, or how we view the evidence based on our beliefs and our experiences. For those of us who have had such spiritually transformative experiences, no proof is necessary. For those of us who haven't, it will depend on how we interpret the facts based on our own beliefs.

I suppose in writing this book, the *onus probandi*, or burden of proof, is on me. This book contains numerous testimonials and anecdotes offering convincing evidence of the validity of the afterlife. We also heard from some well-known experts who have backed up such claims with extensive research. But let's be honest: Science demands much more than the anecdotal evidence we've seen in this book.

Scientific evidence is data that either supports or counters a particular theory. A scientific theory must be based on observable, verifiable facts. As these theories are tested, they can then be modified, improved, proven, or rejected in time. As an example, Isaac Newton developed a theory to explain how objects move both in space and here on Earth. Then Albert Einstein improved it years later with his theory of general relativity.

When consistency is observed and obtained, the idea or hypothesis then becomes a theory. It seems then that science has little use for anecdotal evidence, but to say that something can't be real because it cannot be observed in a lab is biased and close-minded.

Skeptics often say that evidence pertaining to the metaphysical is largely anecdotal or based on personal experience. For this reason, many say such evidence is invalid or worthless. True, most supernatural evidence is based on personal experiences or eyewitness testimony, but they are not worthless by any means. They are in fact very significant.

Albert Einstein explained this well when he said, "Pure logical thinking cannot yield us any knowledge of the empirical world. All knowledge of reality starts from experience and ends in it." In other words, all knowledge starts with personal experience. Such testimony is real and, yes, does count. If they didn't, eyewitness testimony wouldn't be admissible in a court of law.

I am not by any means claiming that every story should be taken as true. There are three things that should be considered when evaluating whether or not anecdotal evidence is valid:

1. **Volume:** How many people have claimed that such phenomena have taken place? Thousands of deathbed and other paranormal claims have been made throughout history. Hundreds of books have been written on such phenomena.

2. **Believability:** How credible are those making such claims? These accounts are mostly from the people who had them. Many are nurses, doctors, and other medical professionals.

3. **Uniformity:** How regular or similar are these claims? These claims are different but yet so much alike. They are very consistent. For example, the majority report seeing deceased loved ones or religious figures at their deathbed.

Using the VBU (volume, believability, and uniformity) factors, how credible are the stories and testimonials in this book? None of the contributors to this book have been paid. What do they stand to gain from making a fabricated claim?

Skeptics also argue that these claims cannot be tested or repeated in a lab. Consider this: Everything that we see (the Earth, the sun, the stars, and so on) makes up about 5 percent of the mass of the universe. Most of the universe we live in is composed of matter that cannot be observed. An invisible substance (dark matter) makes up 25 percent, and the rest of the universe is composed of what is known as dark energy (70 percent). Therefore, what we consider real is actually a fraction of the universe.

Think about this for a moment: The majority of our universe is composed of dark matter and dark energy—the unseen. Scientists cannot observe this mysterious, invisible matter, yet they know it exists because of its gravitational effects.

The nature of reality will continue to be masked with the mysterious and science will continue to fall short until researchers study the unseen. It is in studying the nonphysical world that science will finally come to fully understand the physical world. Likewise, it is in understanding spiritual experiences, such as deathbed phenomena, that we will come to understand life.

One day I was invited to a party at my friend Holly's house. While there, I was approached by a woman named Lori who introduced herself as a psychic medium. Lori then proceeded to tell me that my deceased Uncle Carmine was there. He wanted me to tell his son that he was with his daughter in-law, Lynn. She told me that other relatives were with Lynn as well and that she was not alone.

I stood there dumbfounded. At that very moment, my Cousin Angelo's wife was fighting for her life. Lynn was always a heavy smoker and had been diagnosed with lung cancer. Her father in-law, my Uncle Carmine, died years earlier. Everything Lori (a complete stranger) told me was correct.

One week later, I had a very strange but vivid dream. In it, I saw myself walking down a dimly lit hospital corridor. Finally, I came to this room and walked in and saw someone laying in the hospital bed. I was shocked when I realized it was my deceased Uncle Tony. He had his eyes closed. I was surprised to see my uncle and screamed, "Uncle Tony! What are you doing here? You are dead and buried."

At that point, my Uncle Tony looked at me and said, "Of course, I'm not dead. Do you know how much I miss you?" He looked back at me with this smug look on his face as though he was saying, "You of all people know that I'm not dead."

My uncle was a second father to me and I was so ecstatic to see him. I then became aware that there was someone else in the room with us but I had no idea who. It felt as though my Uncle Tony wanted me to know that we were not alone.

The dream was so real and I knew what I had experienced is what I call a visit from heaven. I woke up that morning and couldn't get the whole experience out of my head. I even went on to my Visits from Heaven Facebook group and wrote about the dream. I told the members of my group that although I didn't know who it was, I was certain that someone else was in that hospital room with me and my Uncle Tony.

About an hour later, I had my answer. My cousin Maria (my Uncle Tony's daughter) called to tell me that Lynn had passed that night. Now everything made perfect sense. My uncle was letting me know that he was there with Lynn to help her transition. Lynn was indeed not alone.

I often wonder who will be there to escort me to the Other Side. The truth is I won't know until that moment comes. But there is one thing I do know for certain, I will not die alone. None of us will.

As this book has shown, we are never really alone. Not in birth. Not in life. And certainly not in death.

APPENDIX

There Is Life After Death

I will never forget the day I first met my friend Lisa. She had just moved back into town and was waiting outside the entrance of the school for her daughter. I'm not one to go up to strangers but something drew me to her and I introduced myself. My daughter Lia, we later came to find out, was in the same class as her daughter.

Their friendship blossomed and so did ours. As Lisa and I got to know each other, she told me that she was not a churchgoer and did not believe in God. That's fine; people have a right to believe whatever they choose to believe. But then Lisa told me about several spiritual experiences that she had. For example, she had several dream premonitions that later came true. I could not understand how anyone who has had such experiences could not believe in a higher power.

As I got to know Lisa more and more, I was amazed by all the many intuitive and spiritual events that have taken place in her life. So one day I asked her if she believed in spiritual phenomena. Her answer was yes. But I questioned, "Yet, you don't believe in God?"

This led to many long conversations about God and the nature of religion. How can spiritual phenomena take place if there wasn't a God or a higher power allowing it to happen?

Lisa and I also have had several conversations about the afterlife. I would often tell her that there was life after death and how she would someday be surprised. Now fast forward several months and Lisa was on vacation in Sarasota, Florida, shopping. While in the store, she came across a purple anklet. Although there were multiple colors, she was drawn to the purple one. Each color had meaning and according to the chart, this particular one represented faith.

She was not happy with the color's affiliation but decided to buy it anyway and put it on. That night back at the hotel, Lisa woke up abruptly to what she described as a crackling or pulsating sound. It was pitch black in the room and her husband was sound asleep next to her, while her two daughters slept in the bed next to them.

Straight ahead at the foot of the bed in front of the TV was what she described as vibrating energy in an odd lightning shape. "It was a zig-zagged shape, about 2 feet by 3 feet. I was shocked and just stared at it. Then all of a sudden, I heard very clearly, *There is life after death!*

"When I say I heard it, I mean in thought or telepathically. Then as soon as I heard it, there was this very loud pop and it was gone."

The popping sound was so loud that Lisa was surprised her family did not wake up. But no one else in the room heard or saw anything.

The next day, Lisa called me from the balcony of the hotel to tell me what had happened the night before. As Lisa spoke animatedly about what happened, I smiled to myself. Were the angels backing up what I had told Lisa so many times?

Suddenly, Lisa stopped talking to tell me that a bunch of dragonflies unexpectedly appeared, surrounding her on the 11th-floor balcony. "Aren't dragonflies a symbol of the afterlife?" she asked.

"Yes," I told her. "Yes, they are."

BIBLIOGRAPHY

Alexander, Eben. *Proof of Heaven: A Neurosurgeon's Journey Into the Afterlife*. New York: Simon and Schuster Paperbacks, 2012.

Barbato, Michael. *Reflections of a Setting Sun*. Australia: Michael Barbato, 2009.

Barrett, Sir William. *Deathbed Visions: How the Dead Talk to the Dying*. United Kingdom: White Crow Books, 2011.

Cap, Annie. *Beyond Goodbye: An Extraordinary True Story of a Shared Death Experience*. United Kingdom: Annie Cap, 2011.

Clark, Nancy. *Divine Moments: Ordinary People Having Spiritually Transformative Experiences*. Fairfield, Iowa: 1st World Publishing, 2012.

Cobbe, Frances Power. *The Peak in Darien: An Octave of Essays*. Boston: Geo. H. Ellis, 1882.

Dossey, Larry. *The Power of Premonitions: How Knowing the Future Can Shape Our Lives*. New York: Dutton Adult, 2009.

Fenwick, Dr. Peter, and Elizabeth Fenwick. *The Art of Dying*. London: Continuum, 2008.

Greyson, Bruce. "Seeing Dead People Not Known to Have Died: 'Peak in Darien' Experiences." *Anthropology and Humanism* 35 (2010): 159–171.

Haig, Dr. Scott. "The Brain: The Power of Hope." *Time,* 29 (2007).

Huxley, Julian. "The Creed of a Scientific Humanist" in *The Meaning of Life*. Oxford: Oxford University Press, 2000.

Jones, Marie D. *PSIence: How New Discoveries in Quantum Physics and New Science May Explain the Existence of Paranormal Phenomena.* Wayne, N.J.: Career Press, Inc., 2007.

Kerr, Dr. Christopher W., Dr. James P. Donnelly, Scott T. Wright, Sarah M. Kuszczak, Anna Banas, Dr. Pei C. Grant, and Debra L. Luczkiewicz. "End-of-Life Dreams and Visions: A Longitudinal Study of Hospice Patients' Experiences." *Journal of Palliative Medicine* 17 (2014).

Kessler, David. *Visions, Trips, and Crowded Rooms: Who and What You See Before You Die.* United Kingdom: Hay House, Inc., 2010.

Kircher, Pamela M. *Love is the Link: A Hospice Doctor Shares her Experience of Near-Death and Dying.* Pagosa Springs, Colo.: Awakenings Press, 2013.

Koedam, Ineke. *In the Light of Death: Experiences on the Threshold Between Life and Death.* United Kingdom: White Crow Books, 2015.

Lerma, Dr. John. *Learning from the Light.* Wayne, N.J.: The Career Press, Inc, 2009.

Moody Jr., Dr. Raymond. *Glimpses of Eternity: Sharing a Loved One's Passage from his Life to the Next.* New York: Guideposts, 2010.

Nahm, Dr. Michael, and Bruce Greyson. "The Death of Anna Katharina Ehmer: A Case Study in Terminal Lucidity." *Omega Journal of Death and Dying* 68 (2013–14): 77–88.

"Religion and the Unaffiliated," *Pew Research Center,* 9 July 2012.

Sartori, Dr. Penny. *The Wisdom of Near Death Experiences: How Understanding NDEs Can Help Us Live More Fully.* United Kingdom: Watkins Publishing Ltd.

Song, Daegene. "Consciousness Does Not Compute (and Never Will), Says Korean Scientist," *PR Newswire,* 5 May 2015.

Taylor, Dr. Steve. "The Puzzle of Consciousness." *Psychology Today,* 4 (2014).

Varga, Josie. *Divine Visits.* Virginia Beach, Va.: 4th Dimension Press, 2010.

————. *Visits from Heaven.* Virginia Beach, Va.: 4th Dimension Press, 2009.

————.*Visits to Heaven.* Virginia Beach, Va.: 4th Dimension Press, 2011.

Whitfield, Barbara Harris. *The Natural Soul.* Pittsburgh, Penn.: SterlingHouse Publisher, Inc., 2009.

Wills-Brandon, Dr. Carla. *One Last Hug Before I Go: The Mystery and Meaning of Deathbed Visions.* Deerfield Beach, Fla.: Health Communications, Inc., 2000.

NOTES

Introduction

1. Barrett, *Deathbed Visions*, 24.
2. Ibid., 27–28.
3. Wills-Brandon, *One Last Hug Before I Go*, 162.
4. *http://hallucinations.enacademic.com/437/deathbed_vision.*
5. *www.hospicebuffalo.com/files/9313/9144/3823/Kerr_CW_2014_-_EOL_Dreams_and_Visions_I_Quant_RE.pdf*
6. *https://en.wikipedia.org/wiki/American_Society_for_Psychical_Research.*
7. *www.brainyquote.com/quotes/quotes/j/jamesantho153365.html.*

Comatose to Lucid Right Before Death

1. Greyson and Nahm, "Death of Anna Ehmer," 77–88.
2. Ibid.
3. Batthyany, interview with the author, 2016.
4. Ibid.
5. *www.researchgate.net/publication/51497433_Terminal_lucidity_A_review_and_a_case_collection.*
6. *http://content.time.com/time/printout/0,8816,1580392,00.html."*
7. Haig, "Power of Hope," 29.
8. Ibid.
9. Ibid.
10. Ibid.

The Question of Consciousness

1. *www.unknowncountry.com/news quantum-physicist-consciousness-arises-outside-brain* and *http://caravantomidnight.com/quantum-physicist-consciousness-arises-outside-of-the-brain/.*

2. Alexander, *Proof of Heaven*, 8.
3. Ibid.
4. Ibid.
5. Ibid.
6. Ibid.
7. Ibid.
8. *www.psychologytoday.com/blog/out-the-darkness/201411/the-puzzle -consciousness.*

"Peak in Darien" Experiences: Dr. Bruce Greyson

1. Cobbe, *Peak in Darien.*
2. Greyson, "Seeing Dead People," 159–171.
3. Ibid.
4. Greyson, interview with the author, 2016.
5. Ibid.

Understanding the Dying Process

1. *www.near-death.com/science/experts/melvin-morse.html.*
2. Morse, "Everything Guide to Evidence."

Life's Mysteries Are Revealed in Its Final Moments

1. Barbato, interview with the author, 2016.
2. Ibid.
3. Ibid.
4. Barbato, *Reflections of the Setting.*
5. Barbato, interview with the author, 2016.
6. Ibid.
7. Ibid.
8. Ibid.

Dying to See Angels: Dr. John Lerma

1. *www.near-death.com/science/evidence/people-born-blind-can-see-during -nde.html.*

Beyond Goodbye: A Shared Death Experience

1. Moody, *Glimpses of Eternity*, 11.
2. Ibid.

Atmospheric Changes

1. Fenwick, *Art of Dying*.
2. Varga, *Visits to Heaven*, 348–350.

Spiritual but Not Religious

1. *www.intuition.org/txt/moody.htm.*
2. *www.pewforum.org/2012/10/09/nones-on-the-rise-religion/.*
3. *www.intuition.org/txt/moody.htm.*
4. Kessler, *Visions, Trips, and Crowded Rooms*, 23.
5. Ibid., 24.
6. Ibid., 161–162.

Final Thoughts

1. Fenwick, *Art of Dying*, 239
2. Ibid., 241–242.

INDEX

Acute events, 161-168

Addiction, 45

Afterlife
communication, 40-41
research, 39-45

Alexander, Dr. Eben, 31-33

Alternate realities, 100

Altruism, 36

Alzheimer's disease, 26

Angels, 17, 23, 24, 65, 82, 103,
105-111, 117, 140, 146, 160

Apparitions, 131

Art of Dying, The, 131, 170

Atmosphere, 24, 131

Awareness, nearing death,
155-156

Barbato, Dr. Michael, 68-72

Barrett,
Florence E., 19-20
William, 19-20, 44

Batthyany, Alexander, 26-27

Bede, 18

Belief structures, 13

Beliefs, religious, 25

Believability, 172

Beyond Goodbye, 117

Bigham, Cindy, 50-52

Borysenko, Dr. Joan, 72-77

Brain integrity, 26

Call of the Wild, The, 121-122

Callanan, Maggie, 155

Calvert, Melanie, 94-95

Cap, Annie, 116, 117-120

Carter, Jennifer, 147-150

Chalmers, David, 35

Changes, atmospheric, 24, 131

Children, death and, 14, 42, 61

Clairvoyance, 83

Clarity, mental, 25

Clark, Nancy, 150-154

Cobbe, Frances, 52

Communication, afterlife, 40-41

Consciousness after death, 13

Consciousness Explained, 35

Consciousness, 18, 30-38, 75, 128

Consistency, 14

Cooper, Sharon, 110

Davis, Bill, 132-134

De Chardin, Pierre Teilhard, 156

Death,

    children and, 14, 42, 61

    consciousness after, 13

Death-related sensory

    experiences (DRSEs), 64

Dennett, Daniel, 35

DiBernardo, Toni, 139

Divine Moments, 150

Divine Visits, 15

Donnelly, James P., 22

Dossey, Larry, 85

Dream state, 140-141

Dreaming, prophetic, 83-91

Dreams, 24

Dying process, the, 56-63

Ehmer, Anna Katharina, 25-26

Einstein, Albert, 69, 171

Enduring Love, 46

Energy, 38

Events, acute, 161-168

Evidential deathbed visit

    (EDV), 58

Extra-sensory perception

    (ESP), 83

Fear, 18, 21, 41-44, 71-72, 97, 99,

    127, 159, 169

Fear of death, 13, 22, 33, 43, 44,

    53, 58, 61, 117, 170

Fenwick, Dr. Peter, 15, 44, 96,

    97, 131, 170

Fenwick, Elizabeth, 131

Final Gifts, 154

Freud, Sigmund, 14

Froude, James Anthony, 25

Galilei, Galileo, 68

Gateway, 24

Glimpses of Eternity, 116

Grant, Pei C., 22

Greyson, Dr. Bruce, 25, 52-55, 78

Haig, Dr. Scott, 28-29

Hallucinations, 20-21, 44, 55, 59,

    64-65, 70, 121, 148, 157, 161

Hamlet, 82

Happich, Friedrich, 25-26

Haraldsson, Dr. Erlendur, 21, 44

Hay, Louise, 159

Hearing, 24

Holmes, J.H., 36

Human thought, 31

Impending journey, 123

Integrity, brain, 26

International Association for

Near-Death Studies (IANDS),

    54, 58

Intuition, 85

James, William, 22-23

Jesus, 23, 68, 103, 104, 105, 107, 109, 110, 160, 162, 163, 164

Journey, impending, 123

Kalmus, Natalie, 53

Keats, John, 52

Kelley, Patricia, 155

Kennedy, Margaret, 130-131

Kerling, Betty J., 100-102

Kerr, Christopher W., 22

Kessler, David, 159-160

Kircher, Dr. Pamela, 161-168

Koedam, Ineke, 95-100

Kubler-Ross, Dr. Elizabeth, 111, 159

Landberg, Mary, 45-46

Lazaro, Patricia, 79-81

Learning From the Light, 105, 106

Lerma, Dr. John, 105-111

Life After Life, 117, 157

Life support, 78, 137

Life, meaning of, 13

Light of Death, In the, 96

London, Jack, 121

Loranger, John, 78

Lucidity, terminal, 25-30

Luczkiewicz, Debra, 22

Make Up Your Mind to Be Happy, 99

Martin, Jennie Taylor, 91-93

Mary, 23, 107-108, 147

McGinn, Colin, 35

Meaning of life, 13

Mental clarity, 25

Mental reasoning, 26

Mistakes, 164

Moody, Dr. Raymond, 44, 116, 117, 157-159

Morse, Dr. Melvin, 59

Moshlove, Jeffrey, 158

Murray, Pamela, 124-127

Nahm, Michael, 25

Nature of reality, the, 32

Near-death experiences (NDEs), 23, 27, 32, 54, 56, 59-61, 78, 85, 110, 116, 117, 157, 161-168

Nearing death awareness, 155-156

One Last Hug Before I Go, 38

Osis, Karlis, 21

Out-of-body experiences (OBEs), 117

Paranoia, 21, 148

Paranormal phenomena, 18, 42, 125, 172

Parker, Shelley E., 83-91

Parnia, Dr. Sam, 156

Patterns, 14

Peak in Darien experiences, 52-55

Perception, 26, 30

Perry, Paul, 116

Peters, William, 120-124

Phillips, Dr. Betty, 154-157

Piscitella-Musolino, Anna, 142-143

Power of Premonitions, The, 84

Premonitions, 83-85

Proof of Heaven, 32

Prophetic dreaming, 83-91

Puma Punku, 29

Quantum physics, 38

Realities, alternate, 100

Reality, the nature of, 32

Reasoning, mental, 26

Redmond, Nancy, 102-103

Reflections of a Setting Sun, 70, 71

Religious beliefs, 24

Research, afterlife, 39-45

Responsiveness, 25

Reunions, 157

Reyes, Dolores, 127-130

Ring, Kenneth, 110

Robinson, Lakisa, 103-104

Sagan, Carl, 170

Sartori, Dr. Penny, 56

Sawyers, Peggy, 93

Sciberras, Carrie, 137-138

Science of consciousness, 13

Scott, Lewis Everett, 144

Shakespeare, William, 82

Shared-death experience (SDE), 115-124

Sheltmire, Cindy, 143-146

Sixth sense, 83

Society for Psychical Research, 20, 21

Song, Daegene, 31

Spirit, 18

Spirits, 131

Spiritual but not religious (SBNR), 157-160

Spiritually transformative experiences (STEs), 169-170

Synchronicity, 24

Taylor, Steven, 33

Telepathy, 36, 83

Tennis, Alice, 146-147

Terminal illness, near-death experiences and, 161-168

Terminal lucidity, 25-30

Tesla, Nikola, 38

Thinking Allowed, 158

Tunnel, 117

Understanding the dying process, 56-63

Uniformity, 172

Visions, Trips, and Crowded Rooms, 159

Visits to Heaven, 23, 117, 132

Washington, George, 82

Whitfield, Barbara Harris, 78-79

Wills-Brandon, Carla, 21, 38-45

Wisdom of Near-Death Experiences, The, 56

Wittneben, Wilhelm, 25-26

ABOUT THE AUTHOR

A Call From Heaven is best-selling author Josie Varga's sixth title. She is also the author of *Divine Visits, Visits to Heaven, Make Up Your Mind to Be Happy, Visits From Heaven,* and *Footprints in the Sand: A Disabled Woman's Inspiring Journey to Happiness.* Besides being a former communications consultant, she also served as the director of communications and editor for a trade association.

As a speaker, Josie helps the bereaved by sharing her message that life never ends and love never dies. She also teaches others to focus on the positive, explaining why happiness is all a matter of how we think.

She has several other book projects in the works and is also working on a television pilot based on her book *Visits From Heaven.* She also has a popular group on Facebook based on *Visits From Heaven* that provides a forum for people to share their experiences.

Her books are available online or wherever books are sold. For more information, visit *www.josievarga.com* or her blog at *http://josie varga.wordpress.com/.*

If you have a spiritual experience to share, please contact Josie at josievarga@comcast.net.